REBOUND
STRONG

REBOUND STRONG

*Hope and Strength for Life's
Toughest Challenges*

DAVID YOUNG

Wind Runner Press
Round Rock, Texas

Rebound Strong
Copyright © 2012 by David Young

Published by Wind Runner Press
P.O. Box 5730, Round Rock, TX 78683
Visit our Web sight at ReboundStrong.com

All rights reserved. No part of this book may be reproduced or transmitted in any form or by any means, electronic or mechanical, including photocopying, recording, or by an information storage and retrieval system – except by a reviewer who may quote brief passages in a review to be printed in a magazine, newspaper, or on the Web – without permission from the publisher.

Scripture taken from the HOLY BIBLE, NEW INTERNATIONAL VERSION.® Copyright © 1973, 1978, 1984 International Bible Society. Used by permission of Zondervan Publishing House.

Rebound strong : hope and strength for life's toughest challenges / [compiled by] David Young. –1st ed.
ISBN-13: 978-1-936179-08-4
ISBN-10: 1-936179-08-3
Library of Congress Control Number: 2011946245
1. Success–Quotations, maxims, etc. 2. Conduct of life–Quotations, maxims, etc. I. Young, David, 1957-
PN6084.S78B74 2012   646.7
                                                  QBI09-600147

Dedication

To the memory of my father and mother, Dayton and Mina, who taught me the value of hard work. And to my wife, Christina, who showed me the power of love.

Introduction

Does your situation seem hopeless? Does it look like there's no way out? Perhaps your doctor gave you bad news. Maybe a family situation is out of control. Or perhaps you're struggling to buy groceries and pay your bills. If so, don't give up. Former Senate chaplain Peter Marshall reminds us that "God will not permit any troubles to come upon us, unless He has a specific plan by which great blessing can come out of the difficulty."

Others have triumphed over adversity, and you can too. How did they do it? They'll share their secrets in *Rebound Strong*. For each day of the year, this book provides four great quotes that will help you overcome life's toughest challenges. You'll learn how to conquer difficulties, and you'll gain hope and strength for the journey. You can triumph over adversity and live a happy and fulfilled life.

January 1

God Will Provide

When we call on God, He bends down His ear to listen, as a father bends down to listen to his little child.
— *Elizabeth Charles*

God's hand is not so short that He cannot save, nor is His ear so heavy that He cannot hear. Whether you see Him or not, He is at work in your life this very moment.
— *Charles Swindoll*

Never be afraid to trust an unknown future to a known God.
— *Corrie ten Boom*

We can depend on God to fulfill His promise, even when all the roads leading to it are closed.
— *Matthew Henry*

January 2

The Adversity Advantage
I am grateful for all my problems. I became stronger and more able to meet those that were still to come.
— *J.C. Penney*

After crosses and losses men grow humbler and wiser.
— *Benjamin Franklin*

People striving, being knocked down and coming back, that's what builds character in a man.
— *Tom Landry*

Life is not about waiting for the storm to pass; it's about learning to dance in the rain.
— *Anonymous*

January 3

The Power of Humility
Those who first accept the silence of obscurity are best qualified to handle the applause of popularity.
— *Charles Swindoll*

When God wants to do His great works He trains somebody to be quiet enough and little enough, then He uses that person.
— *J. Hudson Taylor*

The humble man feels no jealously or envy. He can praise God when others are preferred and blessed before him. He can bear to hear others praised while he is forgotten.
— *Andrew Murray*

When someone asked Saint Francis of Assisi why and how he could accomplish so much, he replied: "The Lord looked down from heaven upon the earth and said, 'Where can I find the weakest, the littlest, the poorest man on the face of the earth?' Then He saw me and said, 'I will work through him. He won't be proud of it. He'll see that I am only using him because of his littleness and insignificance.'"
— *C. Reuben Anderson*

January 4

The Power of Commitment
Be of good cheer. Do not think of today's failures, but of the success that may come tomorrow. You have set yourselves a difficult task, but you will succeed if you persevere; and you will find joy in overcoming obstacles. Remember, no effort that we make to attain something beautiful is ever lost.
— *Helen Keller*

The moment you commit and quit holding back, all sorts of unforeseen incidents, meetings and material assistance will rise up to help you. The simple act of commitment is a powerful magnet for help.
— *Napoleon Hill*

Building your foundation even when you aren't winning is a powerful form of commitment. You improve your chances of becoming a winner when you take this long view.
— *Joe Torre*

Don't get caught up with always needing to see instant results from your work. Instead, have faith that there will always be a reaction, because that faith is what allows you to make a lifelong commitment toward goodness instead of always looking for the shortcuts.
— *Russell Simmons*

January 5

The Power of Laughter

We don't laugh because we're happy – we're happy because we laugh.

— *William James*

There is healing power in laughter. It makes us forget, makes us relax and makes us feel like life is worth living again.

— *Art Berg*

Humor is the great thing, the saving thing, after all. The minute it crops up, all our hardnesses yield, all our irritations and resentments slip away, and a sunny spirit takes their place.

— *Mark Twain*

Remember that laughter can brighten a cloudy day, lighten a heavy load and release the tension in a tight moment. Besides, laughter is attractive. Try it and see how much prettier you look. Laughter is appealing.

— *Patsy Clairmont*

January 6

Benefit from Failure
Strong people make as many mistakes as weak people. The difference is that strong people admit them, laugh at them and learn from them. That is how they became strong.

— *Richard Needham*

I ended up learning much more about life by not winning the gold. Don't get me wrong – I'm disappointed I didn't win, and I still struggle at times with anger at God for the way it happened. But the message from Him continues to come through that His loving purpose is being worked out in my life.

— *Dave Johnson*

It's impossible to fail without having been partially successful. You did succeed at overcoming the fear of getting started.

— *Robert Schuller*

No disappointment, setback, trauma or tragedy becomes so devastating that you cannot glean something of value to take with you to the next experience. Successful people learn from everything that happens to them. They become victorious in situations where others see themselves only as victims.

— *Cherie Carter-Scott*

January 7

Faith

Take the first step in faith. You don't have to see the whole staircase, just take the first step.
— *Martin Luther King, Jr.*

Faith like Job's cannot be shaken because it is the result of having been shaken.
— *Abraham Heschel*

Your seed of greatness will not grow without you using your faith to stretch yourself beyond your past limitations.
— *T.D. Jakes*

By faith Abraham, even though he was past age – and Sarah herself was barren – was enabled to become a father because he considered him faithful who had made the promise.
— *Hebrews 11:11*

January 8

Overcome Difficulties
The way you react to adversity is the key to success. People who succeed are the ones who respond the right way in adverse circumstances.
— *Tom Landry, to his players after he was fired as head coach of the Cowboys*

I make the most of all that comes and the least of all that goes.
— *Sara Teasdale*

Most of the significant things done in the world were done by people who were either too busy or too sick. There are few ideal and leisurely settings for the disciplines of growth.
— *Robert Henderson*

The men whom I have seen succeed best in life have always been cheerful and hopeful men, who went about their business with a smile on their faces, and took the changes and the chances of this mortal life like men, facing rough and smooth alike as it came.
— *Charles Kettering*

January 9

Overcome Fear

The most drastic and usually the most effective remedy for fear is direct action.
— *William Burnham*

When you face your fear, most of the time you will discover that it was not really such a big threat after all.
— *Les Brown*

Anyone can conquer fear by doing the things he fears to do, provided he keeps doing them until he gets a record of successful experiences behind him.
— *Eleanor Roosevelt*

Fear is an illusion. You think something is standing in your way, but nothing is really there. What is there is an opportunity to do your best and gain some success. If it turns out my best isn't good enough, then at least I'll never be able to look back and say I was too afraid to try.
— *Michael Jordan*

January 10

Prayer
Heaven is full of answers to prayers for which no one ever bothered to ask.
— *Billy Graham*

We shall come one day to a heaven where we shall gratefully know that God's great refusals were sometimes the true answers to our truest prayer.
— *Peter Forsyth*

Prayer is not designed for the furnishing of God with the knowledge of what we need, but it is designed as a confession to Him of our sense of need.
— *A.W. Pink*

I have been driven to my knees many times by the overwhelming conviction that I had nowhere else to go. My own wisdom and that of all those about me seemed insufficient for that day.
— *Abraham Lincoln*

January 11

The Power of Positive Thinking
Optimism is the faith that leads to achievement. Nothing can be done without hope and confidence.
— *Helen Keller*

Mount Everest, you have defeated me. But I will return. And I will defeat you. Because you can't get any bigger and I can.
— *Sir Edmund Hillary*

You've got to believe in yourself and have a persistent mindset of never giving up, never quitting. If you get any inclination of "You're not good enough," it kills you.
— *Keenan McCardell*

Don't stop believing in yourself because you haven't yet been rewarded with that brass ring. If I had stopped believing in myself, I never would have realized my lifelong dream of making it to the World Series. It took me 4,272 games as a player and a manager to finally get there, the longest wait for anyone in the history of the game.
— *Joe Torre*

January 12

Overcome Weaknesses

Many a humble soul will be amazed to find that the seed it sowed in weakness, in the dust of daily life, has blossomed into immortal flowers under the eye of the Lord.

— *Harriet Beecher Stowe*

I seldom think about my limitations, and they never make me sad. Perhaps there is just a touch of yearning at times, but it is vague.

— *Helen Keller*

It is always upon human weakness and humiliation, not human strength and confidence, that God chooses to build His Kingdom; and that He can use us not merely in spite of our ordinariness and helplessness and disqualifying infirmities, but precisely because of them.

— *James Stewart*

When we come to the end of ourselves, we come to the beginning of God..

— *Billy Graham*

January 13

God Gives Us Power
The same God who empowered Samson, Gideon and Paul seeks to empower my life and your life, because God hasn't changed.
— *Bill Hybels*

God doesn't give us the jobs we're fit for, He fits us for the jobs He gives us.
— *Anonymous*

Because God is all-powerful, you do not have to doubt your ability, strength or resources to complete His assignments for you. He will enable you to accomplish all that He calls you to do.
— *Henry Blackaby*

[God] gives strength to the weary and increases the power of the weak. Even youths grow tired and weary, and young men stumble and fall; but those who hope in the Lord will renew their strength. They will soar on wings like eagles; they will run and not grow weary, they will walk and not be faint.
— *Isaiah 40:29-31*

January 14

When Bad Things Happen
For every single thing that goes wrong in our lives, we have fifty to one hundred blessings.
— *Barbara Johnson*

Life is like the wrong side of a carpet. We see many different colored threads running every which way. They seem to make no sense at all. But one day in this life or thereafter, we will see the right side of the carpet and then we will realize that everything has made a perfect pattern.
— *Hans Wilhelm*

We should not permit our grievances to overshadow our opportunities.
— *Booker T. Washington*

Your reaction to a problem as much as the problem itself will determine the outcome. I have seen people face the most catastrophic problems with a positive mental attitude, turning their problems into creative experience. They turned their scars into stars.
— *Robert Schuller*

January 15

Receiving Criticism
There is a kernel of truth in every criticism. Look for it, and when you find it, rejoice in its value.
— *Dawson Trotman*

Throughout my career, the things I've done best are the things people told me couldn't be done.
— *Ross Perot*

Your strength as an individual depends on how you respond to both criticism and praise. If you let either one have any special effect on you, it's going to hurt.
— *John Wooden*

A great sign of immaturity is to become very angry or hurt at the slightest criticism from others. A mature person profits from criticism.
— *Vince Lombardi*

January 16

Worry

The best cure for worry, depression, melancholy, brooding, is to go deliberately forth and try to lift with one's sympathy the gloom of somebody else.
— *Arnold Bennett*

It is not work that kills me; it is worry. Worry is rust upon the blade.
— *Henry Ward Beecher*

Worry – a god, invisible but omnipotent. It steals the bloom from the cheek and lightness from the pulse; it takes away the appetite, and turns the hair grey.
— *Benjamin Disraeli*

O Father, save me from the depression that comes from accepting every gloomy prediction and every bad news story as though they were the whole truth. May your grace help me not to be anxious about tomorrow, but to live with the trust that enables me to cope with today.

— *Reginald Hollis*

January 17

The Power of Commitment
I always laugh when people praised me as an overnight success. Overnight plus nine years of training, sacrifice, hard work and discipline was more like it.
— *Mary Lou Retton*

My strongest point is my persistence. I never give up in a match. However down I am, I fight until the last ball. My list of matches shows that I have turned a great many so-called irretrievable defeats into victories.

— *Bjorn Borg*

I wrote for twelve years and collected 250 rejection slips before getting any fiction published, so I guess outside reinforcement isn't all that important to me.
— *Lisa Allen*

Doers are willing to break through the barriers of pain that stand between themselves and a goal. The pain barriers might be emotional or physical – or both. Doers realize that any goal of substance is not meant to be achieved easily and they will face severe tests of their patience and determination along the path to fulfillment.

— *Gary Player*

January 18

Overcome Failure

The most important attribute of successful people is not that they always succeed, but that they respond to failure by coming back and redoubling their efforts.
— *Mary Farrell*

In the many years before we won a championship I overcame disappointment by not living in the past. To do better in the future you have to work on the *right now*. Dwelling in the past prevents doing something in the present.
— *John Wooden*

I don't fear failure because I've got the most important ingredients in life at hand – my family and my faith.
— *George W. Bush*

Losing the Super Bowl was a great disappointment. But I learned from my dad to put things in their proper perspective. It's only natural to have setbacks in life. But you deal with them and you move on. If losing the Super Bowl is the greatest disappointment I have in my life, then I will have lived a very blessed life.

— *Drew Bledsoe*

January 19

Renewal

To acquire the habit of reading is to construct for yourself a refuge from almost all the miseries of life.
— *W. Somerset Maugham*

There must be quite a few things a hot bath won't cure, but I don't know many of them.
— *Sylvia Plath*

When we rest at night we relax our muscles, but we also restore energy and balance to our nervous and immune systems. This recharging helps us to feel sharp and responsive, and allows us to problem-solve and retain our critical thinking and decision-making power. It also allows us to ward off illness and disease.
— *Dr. Paul Donahue*

The colors in the sky at sunset, the delicate tints of the early spring foliage, the brilliant autumn leaves, the softly colored grasses and lovely flowers – what painter ever equaled their beauties with paint and brush?
— *Laura Ingalls Wilder*

January 20

Adversity

The great moments, when the world cheers, are not the moments that count. The ones that count are when it's just you, and people have stopped believing in you. Those are the moments that define you.
— *Bob Greene*

I always tried to turn every disaster into an opportunity.
— *John D. Rockefeller*

Conditions are never just right. People who delay action until all factors are favorable do nothing.
— *William Feather*

When starting out, don't worry about not having enough money. Limited funds are a blessing, not a curse. Nothing encourages creative thinking in quite the same way.
— *H. Jackson Brown, Jr.*

January 21

The Power of Confidence
What you think of yourself is much more important than what others think of you.
— *Seneca*

Strike a balance between confidence and humility – enough confidence to know that you can make a real difference, enough humility to ask for help.
— *Carley Fiorina*

You may succeed when others do not believe in you, but never when you do not believe in yourself.
— *Anonymous*

I have to really believe that I can medal, and then I'll do whatever it takes every day to prepare myself for when that time comes. If I don't think I can, then I'm not going to give it that hundred percent or more that I need to give, to suffer. You have to find that line and go just beyond it.
— *Tinker Juarez*

January 22

Giving

Those who bring sunshine to the lives of others cannot keep it from themselves.

— *Sir James Arrie*

If you share your money, you'll always have enough. And if you don't, you'll never have enough.

— *Chi Chi Rodriguez*

He who gives to the poor will lack nothing.

— *Proverbs 28:27*

No matter how little you have in the way of material things, you always have inner bounty to share. You have encouraging words, creative ideas, a sense of humor and the power of prayer. So, even when you feel your luck is running thin, give something away from your bounty within.

— *Dr. Suzanne Zoglio*

January 23

The Power of Change
Progress is impossible without change; and those who cannot change their minds cannot change anything.
— *George Bernard Shaw*

You must adapt to change, and condition yourself to see it as an opportunity to improve yourself, not as a window to failure.
— *Rick Pitino*

Today, loving change, tumult, even chaos is a prerequisite for survival, let alone success.
— *Tom Peters*

Change has a considerable psychological impact on the human mind. To the fearful it is threatening because it means that things may get worse. To the hopeful it is encouraging because things may get better. To the confident it is inspiring because the challenge exists to make things better.
— *King Whitney, Jr.*

January 24

The Power of Faith
Hope is hearing the melody of the future. Faith is to dance to it.
— *Rubem Alves*

Faith clamps down the teeth of God's Word on the seat of the enemy's pants and hangs on until Satan quits.
— *Marilyn Hickey*

By faith Abraham, when called to go to a place he would later receive as his inheritance, obeyed and went, even though he did not know where he was going.
— *Hebrews 11:8*

At a complete disadvantage – because of his smaller size and his substandard equipment – David was still able to achieve what he was able to believe. David was the only man who could defeat Goliath because he was the only one who had the faith for it.
— *T.D. Jakes*

January 25

Financial Freedom
Save a part of your income and begin now, for the man with a surplus controls circumstances, and the man without a surplus is controlled by circumstances.
— *Henry Buckley*

If a person gets his attitude toward money straight, it will help straighten out almost every other area in his life.
— *Billy Graham*

Every family should work for an emergency fund equal to six months' living expenses, and this should be held in safe investments and regarded as a protection and not as a means to make money.
— *Samuel Crowther*

You need to set aside money for savings each month. Not only does it give you a reserve to draw on in emergency situations, it's a key element in smart financial planning and eventual financial freedom. What's more, having a stash of cash at your disposal can give you peace of mind about your finances.
— *Larry Burkett*

January 26

The Adversity Advantage
I would never have amounted to anything were it not for adversity. I was forced to come up the hard way.
— *J.C. Penney*

When you are in the dark, listen, and God will give you a very precious message for someone else when you get into the light.
— *Oswald Chambers*

If I wasn't dyslexic, I probably wouldn't have won the Games. If I had been a better reader, then that would have come easily, sports would have come easily and I never would have realized that the way you get ahead in life is hard work.
— *Bruce Jenner*

The real irony is this: some of the happiest, most joy-filled people I know are people who have been through some of the worst pain in the world. I don't know exactly why that happens, but this is my guess: once we're no longer afraid to feel any feeling that comes our way, we really do become happy, joyous and free.

— *Melody Beattie*

January 27

Forgiveness
We forgive to the extent that we love.
— *François de La Rochefoucauld*

You will never be asked to forgive someone else more than God has already forgiven you.
— *Rick Warren*

He who has not forgiven an enemy has never yet tasted one of the most sublime enjoyments of life.
— *Johann Lavater*

I think that if God forgives us, we must forgive ourselves.
— *C.S. Lewis*

January 28

God's Guidance

God will always give you enough specific directions to do now what He wants you to do. When you need more directions, He gives you more in His timing.
— *Henry Blackaby*

When we put our lives into God's hands and ask Him to direct us, amazing results will follow.
— *Catherine Marshall*

No man, who acts honestly up to the light he has, will be left in the dark.
— *Charles Haddon Spurgeon*

The steps of good men are directed by the Lord. He delights in each step they take. If they fall it isn't fatal, for the Lord holds them with his hand.
— *Psalm 37:23-24 (TLB)*

January 29

Character Required for Success

The essence of God's teaching is that true greatness lies in character, not in ability or position.
— *A.W. Tozer*

Character is not made on the mountain tops of life; it is made in the valleys.
— *Kathryn Kuhlman*

Character is formed by doing the thing we are supposed to do, when it should be done, whether we feel like doing it or not.
— *Father Flanagan*

Character cannot be developed in ease and quiet. Only through experience of trial and suffering can the soul be strengthened, vision cleared, ambition inspired and success achieved.
— *Helen Keller*

❧ January 30

The Power of Commitment

Genius is perseverance in disguise.
— *Mike Newlin*

You may have to fight a battle more than once to win it.
— *Margaret Thatcher*

We fight until they take the last breath out of us.
— *Darryl Talley, former Buffalo Bills linebacker, on coming back from 35-3 to beat the Houston Oilers in a playoff game*

Somehow over the years folks have gotten the impression that Wal-Mart was just this great idea that turned into an over-night success. But our first Wal-Mart store was totally an outgrowth of everything we'd been doing since 1945 – another case of me being unable to leave well enough alone, another experiment. And like most over-night successes, it was about twenty years in the making.
— *Sam Walton*

January 31

Benefit from Failure

The wisest person is not the one who has the fewest failures, but the one who turns failures to best account.

— *Richard Grant*

I failed my way to success.

— *Thomas Edison*

In God's economy, nothing is wasted. Through failure, we learn a lesson in humility which is probably needed, painful though it is.

— *Bill Wilson*

I think you learn a lot more in failures and defeats, many times, than you do in victories. God has those difficult times to teach us and to help us grow. I didn't look at those 27 years as *failure years*. There were things I learned that helped create that Super Bowl win.

— *Tony Dungy*

February 1

Overcome Difficulties

Nothing splendid has ever been achieved except for those who dare to believe that something inside of them was superior to circumstance.
— *Bruce Barton*

If you can't see the bright side of life, polish the dull side.
— *Anonymous*

One great technique to deal with your fears in the face of adversity is to recount past challenges that you have successfully overcome. Your ability to manage present circumstances is improved when you recall past fears that were never ultimately realized.
— *Art Berg*

I have had more than half a century of such happiness. A great deal of worry and sorrow, too, but never a worry or sorrow that was not offset by a purple iris, a lark, a bluebird or a dewy morning glory.
— *Mary Bethune*

February 2

The Power of Courage
The men who have done big things are those who were not afraid to attempt big things, who were not afraid to risk failure in order to gain success.
— *B.C. Forbes*

Growth happens within us when we face risk. Head-on. Faith and risk go hand in hand.
— *Charles Swindoll*

Great deeds are usually wrought at great risks.
— *Herodotus*

People who are willing to be unreasonable and unrealistic, and take actions beyond their comfort levels will always advance more quickly than those who *play it safe* or work the *status-quo*.
— *Brian Koslow*

February 3

Resolve Conflict

Try to use conflict as a tool – to learn more about the other person and find a solution that serves both of you. Relationships that endure conflict become stronger and deeper.

— *John Maxwell*

In all debates, let truth be thy aim, not victory, or an unjust interest. And endeavor to gain, rather than to expose thy antagonist.

— *William Penn*

Love is strengthened by working through conflicts together.

— *Anonymous*

I think it takes a bigger man to walk away from a problem than to stay and fight about it. What would you gain from fighting? It's nothing but trouble. If someone wants to be an idiot and wants to get into a fight with you, don't give him the satisfaction. Just let it go. You'll feel better because you will have made the savvier decision.

— *Derek Jeter*

February 4

God's Will

Inside the will of God there is no failure. Outside the will of God there is no success.

— *Benard Edinger*

If you want to hear God's voice clearly and you are uncertain, then remain in His presence until He changes that uncertainty. Often, much can happen during this waiting for the Lord. Sometimes, He changes pride into humility, doubt into faith and peace.

— *Corrie ten Boom*

When we are considering any major change or decision in our lives, we must make certain that our *sensible, practical* plans have first been laid at God's feet. If He is really Lord – the supreme authority of our lives – He must be given veto power over all our designs and schemes.

— *Jack Hayford*

All heaven is waiting to help those who will discover the will of God and do it.

— *J. Robert Ashcroft*

February 5

Career
If nothing else about your job sparks some enthusiasm in you, you can do your work well because it's your job. Your performance in it makes a statement about you. You must take pride in that statement.
— *Dr. Bob Rotella*

Every job has drudgery, whether it is in the home, in the professional school or in the office. The first secret of happiness is the recognition of this fundamental fact.
— *Millicent McIntosh*

Don't let your paycheck determine how you approach your work – or how you feel about yourself.
— *Joe Torre*

All members of the I-work-hard-but-because-I'm-not-up-front-I-never-get-the-credit club, take heart. Our God who rewards in secret will never overlook your commitment.
— *Charles Swindoll*

❧ February 6

Getting Advice

Listen to advice and accept instruction, and in the end you will be wise.

— *Proverbs 19:20*

He who builds to every man's advice will have a crooked house.

— *Danish proverb*

Get good counsel before you begin; and when you have decided, act promptly.

— *Sallust*

Few things lead to defeat more quickly than the feeling that you are fighting alone. Seek counsel with others who fight the same battle. They will often be seeking you.

— *Greg Quinn*

February 7

Overcome Adversity

Every failure, obstacle or hardship is an opportunity in disguise. Success in many cases is failure turned inside out.

— *Mary Kay Ash*

There is an alchemy in sorrow. It can be transmuted into wisdom, which, if it does not bring joy, can yet bring happiness.

— *Pearl Buck*

We have no right to ask when sorrow comes, "Why did this happen to me?" unless we ask the same question for every joy that comes our way.

— *Philip Bernstein*

I don't think of all the misery, but of the beauty that still remains.

— *Anne Frank*

February 8

Great Decisions

The quickest way to cut down on bad decisions is to cut down on rushed decisions.

— *Charles Foster*

When you are tired, it is not wise to make decisions. It is during that time that a mood or a dark place in your soul can easily manipulate your judgment.

— *T.D. Jakes*

Good decisions, financial and otherwise, are marked by peace, not panic.

— *Ron Blue*

Don't wait for everything to be perfect before you're willing to make decisions. If you do, you'll always be waiting, and you'll never move forward in the journey of life. For every major fork in the road, there comes a time when you have to make a choice based on the information you have. Make the best choice you can and then move on.

— *John Maxwell*

February 9

A Good Attitude
Having a good attitude can keep you moving forward no matter what obstacles stand in your way.
— *Pat Williams*

Changing your attitude is always more successful than changing your circumstances. When your attitude is positive and determined, the task at hand is fifty percent completed.
— *Greg Quinn*

We cannot choose the things that will happen to us. But we can choose the attitude we will take toward anything that happens. Success or failure depends on your attitude.
— *Alfred Montapert*

The single most significant decision I can make on a day-to-day basis is my choice of attitude. The attitude I choose keeps me going or cripples my progress. It alone fuels my fire or assaults my hope. When my attitudes are right, there's no barrier too high, no valley too deep, no dream too extreme, no challenge too great for me.
— *Charles Swindoll*

February 10

How to Pray

Beware in your prayers, above everything else, of limiting God, not only by unbelief, but by fancying that you know what He can do. Expect unexpected things above all that we ask or think.

— *Andrew Murray*

In prayer always express willingness to accept God's will. Ask for what you want, but be willing to take what God gives you. It may be better than what you ask for.

— *Norman Vincent Peale*

Prayer is surrender – surrender to the will of God and cooperation with that will. If I throw out a boat hook from a boat and catch hold of the shore and pull, do I pull the shore to me, or do I pull myself to the shore? Prayer is not pulling God to my will, but aligning my will with His.

— *E. Stanley Jones*

Let us then approach the throne of grace with confidence, so that we may receive mercy and find grace to help us in our time of need.

— *Hebrews 4:16*

February 11

Faith

Living a life of faith often requires us to leave things alone.

— *A.B. Simpson*

Sorrow looks back. Worry looks around. Faith looks up.

— *Sir John Mason*

Little faith must have everything very plain or else it cannot move at all; but great faith makes crooked things straight, sees light in the midst of darkness, and gathers comfort out of discouragement.

— *Charles Haddon Spurgeon*

Faith is not a leap in the dark; it is a leap out of darkness into the light.

— *David Reed*

❧ February 12

Failure

No man is worthy to succeed until he is willing to fail.

— *A.W. Tozer*

The men who try to do something and fail are infinitely better than those who try nothing and succeed.
— *Lloyd Jones*

I work continuously within the shadow of failure. For every novel that makes it to my publisher's desk, there are at least five or six that died on the way.
— *Gail Godwin*

There is no disgrace in honest failure; there is disgrace in fearing to fail.

— *Henry Ford*

February 13

When Bad Things Happen

Reflect upon your present blessings, of which every man has many; not on your past misfortunes, of which all men have some.

— *Charles Dickens*

If all misfortunes were laid in one common heap whence everyone must take an equal portion, most people would be contented to take their own and depart.

— *Socrates*

If I have learned anything, I owe it neither to precepts nor to books, but to a few opportune misfortunes. Perhaps the school of misfortunes is the very best.

— *Louise de Choiseul*

Keep a record of the times you've triumphed over misfortune. It will assure you that you can do so again. Remember your moments of joy and happiness. They will serve as a reservoir of strength when you most need it.

— *Leo Buscaglia*

February 14

The Power of Patience

If you have patience, you continue doing things properly every day and sooner or later, success comes.
— *Dr. Bob Rotella*

Patience is bitter, but its fruit is sweet.
— *Aristotle*

Patience means waiting without anxiety.
— *St. Francis de Sales*

God gives us the vision, then He takes us down to the valley to batter us into the shape of the vision, and it is in the valley that so many of us faint and give way. Every vision will be made real if we will have patience.

— *Oswald Chambers*

February 15

Overcome Weaknesses

While one person hesitates because he feels inferior, the other is busy making mistakes and becoming superior.
— *Henry Link*

Admit your weaknesses and establish short-term goals to overcome them.
— *Rick Pitino*

I'd had operations on both feet at the age of thirteen to correct some bone deformities and I'd been in plaster for six months, and when the plaster came off, I had to learn to walk and run properly. A year later I joined the running club, doing the sprints.
— *Anne Audain*

Do just once what others say you can't do, and you will never pay attention to your limitations again.
— *James Cook*

February 16

God Gives Us Power
I believe that God will give us all the strength we need to help us resist in all times of distress. But He never gives it in advance, lest we should rely on ourselves and not on Him alone. A faith such as this should allay all our fears for the future.
— *Dietrich Bonhoeffer*

Do not pray for easy lives, pray to be stronger men. Do not pray for tasks equal to your powers, pray for powers equal to your tasks.
— *Phillips Brooks*

God never gives strength for tomorrow, or for the next hour, but only for the strain of the minute.
— *Oswald Chambers*

It is not my ability, but my response to God's ability, that counts.
— *Corrie ten Boom*

February 17

Benefits of Exercise
When I'm low on energy, exercise recharges me. It also relieves stress. A vigorous workout restores perspective and helps me release concerns that had seemed deserving of worry.
— *Tom Gegax*

Exercise is excellent therapy for depression.
— *George Allen*

People who exercise regularly have fewer illnesses.
— *Bernie Siegel*

Exercising and eating right are two of the most important things you can do to enhance your well-being and keep up with the rush of life's oncoming challenges.
— *Mary Lou Retton*

February 18

God Will Provide

Because God knows and understands all things, He can be trusted to do what is best.
— *Billy Graham*

Fear not, for I have redeemed you; I have summoned you by name; you are mine. When you pass through the waters, I will be with you; and when you pass through the rivers, they will not sweep over you. When you walk through the fire, you will not be burned; the flames will not set you ablaze.
— *Isaiah 43:1-2*

No weapon forged against you will prevail.
— *Isaiah 57:14*

When things happen to us that we don't understand, we can scream, "Why me? Why me, God?" We can allow circumstances to drive us away from God. Or we can do an about-face and run to God and cling to Him and find in Him our security and our hope.
— *Paul Azinger, on being diagnosed with cancer*

February 19

The Adversity Advantage
All the adversity I've had in my life, all my troubles and obstacles, have strengthened me. You may not realize it when it happens, but a kick in the teeth may be the best thing in the world for you.
— *Walt Disney*

Adversity is the diamond dust heaven polishes its jewels with.
— *Robert Leighton*

If those tough times hadn't happened, who's to say I'd be playing in the NFL. It really helped my determination, drive and character. Everybody has overcome something in their lives. It's all about how you take those challenges and use them for the better.
— *Michael Lehan*

Difficult times have helped me understand better than before how infinitely rich and beautiful life is in every way and that many things that one goes worrying about are of no importance whatsoever.
— *Isak Dinesen*

February 20

Friends

Friendship is a great stimulant. Talk your problems over with others. Laugh with them.
— *Napoleon Hill*

Do not make friends who are comfortable to be with. Make friends who will force you to lever yourself up.
— *Thomas Watson*

Friendship makes prosperity more brilliant, and lightens adversity by dividing and sharing it.
— *Cicero*

The friend in my adversity I shall always cherish most. I can better trust those who helped to relieve the gloom of my dark hours than those who are so ready to enjoy with me the sunshine of my prosperity.
— *Ulysses S. Grant*

February 21

Achieve Your Dreams

Break down your problem into bits and it won't overwhelm you. Setbacks won't feel insurmountable. Big dreams will seem within reach.
— *Joe Torre*

Go as far as you can see, and when you get there you will always be able to see farther.
— *Zig Ziglar*

The future belongs to those who see the possibilities before they become obvious.
— *Pat Williams*

That impossible dream you dreamed when you were young but got talked out of, the one you thought you outgrew, might be the key to awakening your genius. That special talent you never followed through on might be an important source of delight, the one you should commit to. That old dream might be the one thing that will bring the magic of meaning to your life.
— *Mark Hansen and Barbara Nichols*

February 22

Opportunities in Disguise

In everybody's lifetime there will come a time when one door will close on you. If you're so concerned with the one that closes, you'll never find the one that's open.
— *Tommy Lasorda, on retiring from the Dodgers*

In the middle of difficulty lies opportunity.
— *Bruce Lee*

Entrepreneurs are simply those who understand there is little difference between obstacle and opportunity and are able to turn both to their advantage.
— *Victor Kiam*

Adversity often produces the unexpected opportunity. Look for it. Appreciate and utilize it.
— *John Wooden*

February 23

Overcome Fear

If you listen to your fears, you will die never knowing what a great person you might have been.
— *Robert Schuller*

Everybody's got fear. Everybody's afraid something bad is going to happen sometime. That's life. But what's important is that you don't let it stop you from doing things, taking risks. Every decision is a risk, every choice leaves a choice behind. You can't let yourself get paralyzed by the fear of what might go wrong.
— *Yogi Berra*

I sought the Lord, and he answered me; he delivered me from all my fears.
— *Psalm 34:4*

Some people get frozen by a fear of failure. They get it from their peers or from just thinking about the possibility of negative results. They might be afraid of looking bad or being embarrassed. I realized that if I was going to achieve anything in life, I had to be aggressive. I had to get out there and go for it.
— *Michael Jordan*

❧ February 24

The Power of Laughter

Laughter can relieve tension, soothe the pain of disappointment and strengthen the spirit for the formidable tasks that always lie ahead.
> — *Dwight D. Eisenhower*

A good laugh heals a lot of hurts.
> — *Madeleine L'Engle*

Were it not for my little jokes, I could not bear the burdens of this office. With the fearful strain that is on me night and day, if I did not laugh I should die.
> — *Abraham Lincoln*

I have seen what a laugh can do. It can transform almost unbearable tears into something bearable, even hopeful.
> — *Bob Hope*

February 25

Overcome Difficulties

You are not judged by the height you have risen, but from the depth you have climbed.
— *Frederick Douglas*

Tough times never last, but tough people do.
— *Robert Schuller*

Mother was of royal African blood. Throughout all her bitter years of slavery, she preserved a queen-like dignity.
— *Mary Bethune*

Real difficulties can be overcome; it is only the imaginary ones that are unconquerable.
— *Theodore Vail*

February 26

Benefit from Failure

The turning point at which you begin to attain success is usually defined by some form of defeat or failure.

— *Napoleon Hill*

The fear of failure is infinitely greater than failure. Failure gets me up earlier the next morning than success. If you get right back to work, yesterday's pain becomes today's inspiration.

— *Neil Simon*

Those who try and fail are much wiser than those who never try for fear of failure.

— *André Bustanoby*

All life is an experiment. The more experiments you make the better. What if they are a little coarse, and you may get your coat soiled or torn? What if you do fail, and get fairly rolled in the dirt once or twice? Up again, you shall never be so afraid of a tumble.

— *Ralph Waldo Emerson*

February 27

The Power of Commitment
When I have a cause I'm committed to, achieving it becomes much more important to me than the obstacles in the way.
— *Marilyn Tam*

Many of life's failures are people who did not realize how close they were to success when they gave up.
— *Thomas Edison*

History has demonstrated that the most notable winners usually encountered heartbreaking obstacles before they triumphed. They won because they refused to become discouraged by their defeats.
— *B.C. Forbes*

The line between failure and success is so fine that we are often on the line and do not know it. How many a man has thrown up his hands at a time when a little more effort, a little more patience, would have achieved success. A little more persistence, a little more effort and what seemed hopeless failure may turn to glorious success.
— *Elbert Hubbard*

February 28

Build Your Faith
The strengthening of faith comes through staying with it in the hour of trial.
— *Catherine Marshall*

Faith given back to us after a night of doubt is a stronger thing, and far more valuable to us than faith that has never been tested.
— *Elizabeth Goudge*

Faith is not conjuring up, through an act of your will, a sense of certainty that something is going to happen. No, it is recognizing God's promise as an actual fact, believing it is true, rejoicing in the knowledge of that truth and then simply resting because God said it.
— *L.B. Cowman*

The important thing is not the size of your faith – it is the One behind your faith – God Himself.
— *Oral Roberts*

February 29

Solving Problems

A problem clearly stated is a problem half solved.
— *Dorthea Brande*

Learning to solve problems is like learning to play baseball. You learn to throw, to catch, to bat, to run bases, to make plays and to execute all sorts of refinements of these basic skills. You do not learn to play baseball. You learn these basic skills separately, and you put them together in new combinations every game.
— *Edward Hodnett*

Sometimes it makes sense to sleep on a problem and not react spontaneously, or out of emotion or anger. But once you've calmed down, it's best to deal with people right away to talk things out.
— *Rick Pitino*

One of the greatest things I love in regard to golf or life in general is how you respond to the question: Do you choose the problem or do you choose the answer? The second you choose the answer, you don't have a problem.
— *Susan Anton*

March 1

Receiving Criticism
Be prepared for people to block you and conspire against you. Even your own family may challenge your ability to choose your own way. You can't always expect those close to you to see your dream.
— *Les Brown*

My mother convinced me to learn to enjoy having people tell me I can't do something. Now it's second nature; I love to prove people wrong.
— *Andre Ware*

A fool shows his annoyance at once, but a prudent man overlooks an insult.
— *Proverbs 12:16*

You can't listen to the critics. You can't let them affect you. You must ignore their message and be totally convinced that once you've found your motive, established your work ethic and begun practicing the proper techniques, you are on your way to being more successful.
— *Rick Pitino*

March 2

Worry

When we worry about going broke, getting sick or losing face, our focus is on ourselves. One way to reduce worrying is to shift gears, and focus on how you can help someone else.

— *Dr. Suzanne Zoglio*

Worry is the antithesis of trust. You simply cannot do both.

— *Elisabeth Elliot*

There is nothing that wastes the body like worry, and one who has any faith in God should be ashamed to worry about anything whatsoever.

— *Mahatma Gandhi*

A man ninety years old was asked to what he attributed his longevity. "I reckon," he said, with a twinkle in his eye, "it's because most nights I went to bed and slept when I should have sat up and worried."

— *Dorothea Kent*

March 3

Adversity

Many a rich father wishes he knew how to give his sons the hardships that made him rich.
— *Robert Frost*

To ease another's heartache is to forget one's own.
— *Abraham Lincoln*

There is no man in this world without some manner of tribulation or anguish, though he be king or pope.
— *Thomas à Kempis*

In every crisis there is a message. Crises are nature's way of forcing change – breaking down old structures, shaking loose negative habits so that something new and better can take their place.
— *Susan Taylor*

March 4

The Power of Action
The difficulties you meet will resolve themselves as you advance. Proceed, and light will dawn, and shine with increasing clearness on your path.
— *Jean d'Alembert*

We generate fears while we sit. We overcome them by action. Fear is nature's warning signal to get busy.
— *Dale Carnegie*

The undertaking of a new action brings new strength.
— *Evenius*

It's the action, not the fruit of the action, that's important. You have to do the right thing. It may not be in your power, may not be in your time, that there'll be any fruit. But that doesn't mean you stop doing the right thing. You may never know what results come from your action. But if you do nothing, there will be no result.
— *Mahatma Gandhi*

March 5

Anger

A wise man controls his temper. He knows that anger causes mistakes.
— *Proverbs 14:29 (TLB)*

When anger enters the mind, wisdom departs.
— *Thomas à Kempis*

How much more grievous are the consequences of anger than the causes of it.
— *Marcus Aurelius Antoninus*

Life is short, so don't waste any of it carrying around a load of bitterness. It only sours your life, and the world won't pay any attention anyway.
— *Pat Dye*

March 6

Courage to Begin

The beginnings of all things are small.

— *Cicero*

Everyone who got where he is had to begin where he was.

— *Robert Louis Stevenson*

Begin to weave and God will give the thread.

— *German proverb*

You don't have to be great to start, but you have to start to be great.

— *Zig Ziglar*

March 7

Certainty of God's Love
No matter what comes your way, no matter how tempted you are to give in to despair, never forget: God's love for you can never be exhausted, for His love is beyond measure.
— *Billy Graham*

God loves you because of who God is, not because of anything you did or didn't do.
— *Reginna Brett*

His pleasure is not in the strength of the horse, nor his delight in the legs of a man; the Lord delights in those . . . who put their hope in his unfailing love.
— *Psalm 147:10-11*

There is no pit so deep that God's love is not deeper still.
— *Corrie ten Boom*

March 8

The Power of Positive Thinking

Always picture *success* no matter how badly things seem to be going at the moment.
— *Norman Vincent Peale*

I have become my own version of an optimist. If I can't make it through one door, I'll go through another door – or I'll make a door. Something terrific will come no matter how dark the present.
— *Joan Rivers*

Don't give up on proper thinking just because it doesn't work one day.
— *Tom Watson*

If you think about disaster, you will get it. Brood about death and you hasten your demise. Think positively and masterfully, with confidence and faith, and life becomes more secure, more fraught with action, richer in achievement and experience.
— *Eddie Rickenbacker*

March 9

Overcome Failure

Success is going from failure to failure without loss of enthusiasm.

— *Sir Winston Churchill*

I learned from my father not to wallow in disappointment. He taught me to use these experiences to fight back – not only for myself, but also in a way that's constructive and beneficial to many others. He was a very generous person and despite his lifetime of disappointments, he was an incredible optimist.

— *Lani Guinier*

Ever tried and failed? No matter. Try again and fail better.

— *Samuel Beckett*

Long before any championships were ever won at UCLA, I came to understand that losing is only temporary and not all-encompassing. You must simply study it, learn from it and try hard not to lose the same way again. Then you must have the self-control to forget about it.

— *John Wooden*

March 10

The Importance of Rest
Resting seems wasteful, extravagant, a luxury a person as busy as we are cannot afford. But really, and here's a paradox, resting is as necessary as breathing if we are to do more than cling to the cliff of life by our fingertips.

— *Kari Kent*

Take rest; a field that has rested gives a beautiful crop.
— *Ovid*

Just as the body becomes exhausted by hard labor and is reinvigorated by rest, so the mind needs its weariness relieved by rest.

— *Maimonides*

Rest has cured more people than all the medicine in the world.

— *Harold Reilly*

March 11

Start Where You Are
The lesson which repeats and constantly enforces is, *look under your foot*. You are always nearer the divine and the true source of your power than you think. The lure of the distant and the difficult is deceptive. The great opportunity is where you are. Do not despise your own place and hour.
— *John Burroughs*

If a man will not do anything until he has solved every difficulty, we had better dig his grave.
— *Charles Haddon Spurgeon*

Who waits until circumstances completely favor his undertaking, will never accomplish anything.
— *Martin Luther*

When we cannot act as we wish, we must act as we can.
— *Terence*

March 12

The Power of Commitment
You just can't beat the person who never gives up.
— *Babe Ruth*

Perseverance means seeing the obstacles for what they are, and then mapping out an alternative route, rather than sitting idly by or throwing in the towel and crawling back to your comfort zone.
— *Mary Lou Retton*

The road to achievement takes time, a long time, but you don't give up. You may have setbacks. You may have to start over. You may have to change your method. You may have to go around, or over, or under. You may have to back up and get another start. But you do not quit. You stay the course.
— *John Wooden*

You learn you can do your best even when it's hard, even when you're tired and maybe hurting a little bit. It feels good to show some courage.
— *Joe Namath*

March 13

Prayer
It's hard to dislike people for whom we pray.
— *H.L. Sidney Lear*

Prayer is not only asking, but an attitude of mind which produces the atmosphere in which asking is perfectly natural.
— *Oswald Chambers*

It may be that he can only sigh, stammer and mutter. But as long as it is a request brought before God, God will hear it and understand it.
— *Karl Barth*

I believe the old cliché, "God helps those who help themselves," is not only misleading but often dead wrong. My most spectacular answers to prayers have come when I was so helpless, so out of control as to be able to do nothing at all for myself.
— *Catherine Marshall*

March 14

The Adversity Advantage
It's only by the hard blows of adverse fortune that character is tooled.

— *Arnold Glasgow*

Whatever the reasons, the fact that I did not get the coaching opportunities I felt I deserved motivated me greatly.

— *Vince Lombardi*

Even if we may not always understand why God allows certain things to happen to us, we can know He is able to bring good out of evil, and triumph out of suffering.

— *Billy Graham*

Do not believe that he who seeks to comfort you lives untroubled among the simple and quiet words that sometimes do you good. His life has much difficulty and sadness and remains far behind yours. Were it otherwise he would never have been able to find those words.

— *Rainer Rilke*

March 15

Find Contentment

Do not spoil what you have by desiring what you don't have; remember that what you now have was once among the things only hoped for.

— *Epicurus*

Contentment is achieved only in the absence of envy.
— *Tim Kimmel*

More than once I heard Mother say, if we couldn't be happy here in this house, we'd never be happy anywhere.

— *Henry Ford*

He who is not contented with little will never be satisfied with much.

— *Thomas Brooks*

March 16

God's Forgiveness

Forgiveness is man's deepest need and God's highest achievement.

— *Horace Bushnell*

When God forgives He forgets. He buries our sins in the sea and puts up a sign on the bank saying, "No fishing allowed."

— *Corrie ten Boom*

The most marvelous ingredient in the forgiveness of God is that He also forgets, the one thing a human being can never do.

— *Oswald Chambers*

Until God can change or lie, He never will bring to mind again the sin of one whom He has pardoned.

— *Charles Haddon Spurgeon*

March 17

Courage

All courage comes from daring to begin.
— *Eugene Ware*

Courage is an inner resolution to go forward in spite of obstacles and frightening situations; cowardice is a submissive surrender to circumstance.
— *Martin Luther King, Jr.*

This is what I found out about religion; it gives you courage to make the decisions you must make in a crisis, and then the confidence to leave the result to a higher power. Only by trust in God can a man carrying responsibility find repose.
— *Dwight D. Eisenhower*

Courage is being scared to death – and saddling up anyway.
— *John Wayne*

March 18

Trust God

Trust the past to God's mercy, the present to God's love and the future to God's providence.
— *St. Augustine*

In quietness and trust is your strength.
— *Isaiah 30:15*

We cannot trust God until we know something about Him. The way to begin is by reading His word.
— *Catherine Marshall*

Trust God to remember you. He won't forget your name. He won't forget your circumstances. He certainly won't forget your prayers. Trust him; he remembers you.

— *Charles Swindoll*

March 19

Ability

The weakest among us has a gift, however seemingly trivial, which is peculiar to him, and which, worthily used, will be a gift also to his race forever.

— *John Ruskin*

The service of the less gifted brother is as pure as that of the more gifted, and God accepts both with equal pleasure.

— *A.W. Tozer*

I cannot do everything, but still I can do something; and because I cannot do everything I will not refuse to do something that I can do.

— *Edward Hale*

If you follow your dream, and faithfully use what God has gifted you with, your gift will open the doors you need to succeed.

— *T.D. Jakes*

March 20

When Bad Things Happen
Never look at what you have lost. Look at what you have left.

— *Robert Schuller*

When life's problems seem overwhelming, look around and see what other people are coping with. You may consider yourself fortunate.

— *Ann Landers*

People grow through experience if they meet life honestly and courageously. This is how character is built.

— *Eleanor Roosevelt*

There's a story about a guy with terrible problems – ten kids, no money – who goes to a rabbi and asks what to do. The rabbi says, get a goat and move it into your house. So the man does as the rabbis says, but life gets worse. So he goes back to the rabbi and says, "What now?" The rabbi says, get rid of the goat, and you'll feel much better.

— *Robert Fulgham*

March 21

Benefit from Failure

Only those who dare to fail greatly can ever achieve greatly.
— *Robert F. Kennedy*

Losing is a learning experience. It teaches you humility. It teaches you to work harder. It's also a powerful motivator.
— *Yogi Berra*

Have you had little else than defeat? This is the way to success. You will pave the road with the rough flints of your failure.
— *Charles Haddon Spurgeon*

I have learned throughout my life as a composer chiefly through my mistakes and pursuits of false assumptions, not by my exposure to founts of wisdom and knowledge.
— *Igor Stravinsky*

March 22

God Gives Us Power
God always gives us strength enough, and sense enough, for everything that He wants us to do.
— *John Ruskin*

The joy of the LORD is your strength.
— *Nehemiah 8:10*

The Christian does not think God will love us because we are good, but that God will make us good because He loves us.
— *C.S. Lewis*

Your servant has killed both the lion and the bear; this uncircumcised Philistine [Goliath] will be like one of them, because he has defied the armies of the living God. The Lord who delivered me from the paw of the lion and the paw of the bear will deliver me from the hand of this Philistine.
— *1 Samuel 17:36-37*

March 23

The Power of Confidence

The higher your confidence, the faster other people's doubts about you will evaporate.
— *Brian Koslow*

The ones who believed in themselves the most were the ones who won.
— *Florence Griffith-Joyner*

If you have confidence, you have patience.
— *Ilie Natase*

One thing I learned the hard way was that it doesn't pay to get discouraged. Keeping busy and making optimism a way of life can restore your faith in yourself.
— *Lucille Ball*

March 24

Help Others
Turn enemies into friends by doing something nice for them.
— *H. Jackson Brown, Jr.*

Our own rough edges become smooth as we help a friend smooth her edges.
— *Sue Ebaugh*

Help other people cope with their problems, and your own will be easier to cope with.
— *Norman Vincent Peale*

Lord, grant that I may seek to comfort rather than to be comforted; to understand rather than be understood; to love rather than be loved, for it is by forgetting self that one finds. It is by forgiving that one is forgiven.
— *Mother Teresa*

March 25

The Power of Patience

True patience is waiting without worrying.
— *Anonymous*

Be patient in little things. Learn to bear the everyday trials and annoyances of life quietly and calmly, and then, when unforeseen trouble or calamity comes, your strength will not forsake you.
— *William Plummer*

Patience with others is love, patience with self is hope, patience with God is faith.
— *Adel Bestavros*

But these things I plan won't happen right away. Slowly, steadily, surely, the time approaches when the vision will be fulfilled. If it seems slow, do not despair, for these things will surely come to pass. Just be patient! They will not be overdue a single day!
— *Habakkuk 2:3 (TLB)*

March 26

Overcome Difficulties
In life, one goes through all types of adversity. Daddy taught us that we're going to succeed some days and we're going to fail some days and that's how life is. Success is being able to overcome adversity.
— *Martin Luther King III*

Measure the size of obstacles against the size of God.
— *Beth Moore*

A wise man doesn't concern himself with things he can't control.
— *Calvin Peete*

Although Dad suffered terrible setbacks and sorrows – deaths of two daughters, loss of his beloved farm, financial hardships during the Great Depression – he never complained, criticized or compared himself to others who were better off. Through it all he made the best of what he had and was thankful for it.
— *John Wooden*

March 27

Learning

A man learns to skate by staggering about making a fool of himself; indeed, he progresses in all things by making a fool of himself.
— *George Bernard Shaw*

There is no quick way to learn; the only teacher is experience.
— *Forrest Gregg*

Skill to do comes of doing.
— *Ralph Waldo Emerson*

We should welcome awkwardness when we're creating a new habit; it's the sign our brain is creating a pathway that will eventually make us proficient.
— *M.J. Ryan*

March 28

Be Grateful

The best things are nearest: breath in your nostrils, light in your eyes, flowers at your feet, duties at your hand, the path of God just before you.
— *Robert Louis Stevenson*

Cultivate a grateful heart, and you will see blessings where others see curses. You will also likely have better mental health than most and will enjoy life more.
— *M. Scott Peck*

Make a list each day of all that you are grateful for, so that you can stay conscious daily of your blessings. Do this especially when you are feeling as though you have nothing to feel grateful for.
— *Cherie Carter-Scott*

Gratitude. More aware of what you have than what you don't. Recognizing the treasure in the simple – a child's hug, fertile soil, a golden sunset. Relishing in the comfort of the common – a warm bed, a hot meal, a clean shirt.
— *Max Lucado*

March 29

The Secret to Happiness
Try to be happy in this very present moment; don't wait for a better day.
— *Thomas Fuller*

Happiness is different from pleasure. Happiness has something to do with struggling and enduring and accomplishments.
— *George Sheenan*

When you're not thinking about yourself, you're usually happy.
— *Al Pacino*

Paraplegics and lottery winners do not differ significantly in their degree of reported happiness. If you will cease comparing yourself and your success with others and learn to attend more fully to the simple joyful moments of life, you are more likely to feel sweetly successful.
— *Dr. Paul Pearsall*

March 30

Illness

Nothing is more essential in the treatment of serious disease than the liberation of the patient from panic and foreboding.
— *Norman Cousins*

Franklin's illness proved a blessing in disguise, for it gave him strength and courage he had not had before.
— *Eleanor Roosevelt, on her husband's inability to walk as a result of polio*

Illness knocks a lot of nonsense out of us; it induces humility, cuts us down to size. Only when the gate grows narrow do some people discover their soul, their God, their life work.
— *Louis Bisch*

Show me a patient who is able to laugh and play, who enjoys living, and I'll show you someone who is going to live longer. Laughter makes the unbearable bearable and a patient with a well developed sense of humor has a better chance of recovery than a stolid individual who seldom laughs.
— *Dr. Bernie Siegel*

March 31

A Happy Marriage
Never go to bed angry. Say what annoys you, then finish with "I love you." Trust me, it makes the morning brighter.
— *Joan Rivers*

Couples who abandon ship the first time it enters a storm miss the calm beyond. And the rougher the storms weathered together, the deeper and stronger real love grows.
— *Ruth Bell Graham*

Expectations can easily hurt a marriage because the more we expect from our spouses, the more we are likely to take them for granted and the more we are likely not to feel grateful for all the good things they do.
— *Dennis Prager*

It takes two people to have a marriage, but only one is necessary to change it. We end up feeling helpless in our marriages because we can't control our partners. The truth is that we need only learn to control ourselves.
— *Melvyn Kinder and Connell Cowan*

April 1

Overcome Adversity
The cure for grief is motion.
> — *Elbert Hubbard*

Pain is temporary, but quitting is forever.
> — *Lance Armstrong*

Try as we may, none of us can be free of conflict and woe. Even the greatest men have had to accept disappointments as their daily bread. The art of living lies less in eliminating our troubles than in growing with them.
> — *Bernard Baruch*

Believe, when you are most unhappy, that there is something for you to do in the world. So long as you can sweeten another's pain, life is not in vain.
> — *Helen Keller*

April 2

God Will Provide

You turned my wailing into dancing; you removed my sackcloth and clothed me with joy.

— *Psalm 30:11*

Just as God did not choose you when you are high, He will not abandon you when you are low.

— *John Flavel*

God has not promised to deliver us from trouble, but He has promised to go with us through the trouble.

— *Billy Graham*

When we place our dependence in God, we are unencumbered, and we have no worry. This confidence, this sureness of action, is both contagious and an aid to the perfect action. The rest is in the hands of God – and this is the same God, gentlemen, who has won all His battles up to now.

— *Vince Lombardi*

April 3

When You Lose

If you can meet success and failure and treat them both as imposters, then you are a balanced man, my son.
— *Rudyard Kipling*

Never equate losing with failure.
— *Arthur Ashe*

If I lose, I'll walk away and never feel bad. Because I did all I could, there was nothing more to do.
— *Joe Frazier*

It ain't like losing a leg.
— *Billy Joe Patton, on narrowly losing the Masters at Augusta in 1954*

Rebound Strong

April 4

Faith

There is no limit to the inexhaustible power of God, and an *atom of faith* can blast a whole range of material mountains.

— *Howard Carter*

Often God's answers are not the answers we're looking for, and it's important that we arrive at a place in our faith where we are able to accept whatever response He gives us.

— *Mary Lou Retton*

If you have worry, you don't have faith, and if you have faith, you don't have worry.

— *Jack Coe*

Not one of us finds it easy to put our problems into God's hands completely. But only in that way does our trust in Him grow.

— *Catherine Marshall*

April 5

Forget the Past
Regardless of your past, your future is a clean slate.
— *Anonymous*

Let the past go, but hang on to the things it taught you.
— *Pat Williams*

The past is history. Make the present good, and the past will take care of itself.
— *Knute Rockne*

Having loosened our grip on the past, we are free to reach for the future.
— *Ann Clark*

April 6

Debt

To have just finished repaying all one's debts. Ah, is this not happiness?

— *Chin Shengt'an*

The Bible discourages debt because it presumes upon the future – and on God.

— *Ron Blue*

Think what you do when you run debt; you give to another power over your liberty. If you cannot pay at the time, you will be ashamed to see your creditor; will be in fear when you speak to him; will make poor, pitiful, sneaking excuses, and by degrees come to lose your veracity, and sink into base, downright lying; for the second vice is lying, the first is running in debt.

— *Benjamin Franklin*

If you're already in debt and you didn't get there in one year, you probably won't get out in one year. But you can get out. It's a matter of self-discipline and desire.

— *Larry Burkett*

April 7

The Adversity Advantage
Difficulties mastered are opportunities won.
— *Sir Winston Churchill*

God loves us in good times and bad. But He is even more real in our lives when we are having tough times.
— *Joe Gibbs*

I found this out about a tragedy: it either leaves you diminished or enhanced. If you face up to it, if you make the best of it, you're a better person. You appreciate love. You appreciate life. You appreciate all of the things of being with people.
— *Art Linkletter, on the LSD death of his daughter and fatal car crash of his son*

Strength does not come from winning. Your struggles develop your strengths. When you go through hardships and decide not to surrender, that is strength.
— *Arnold Schwarzenegger*

April 8

The Power of Commitment

Success is not measured by what a man accomplishes, but by the opposition he has encountered, and the courage with which he has maintained the struggle against overwhelming odds.

— *Charles Lindbergh*

The urge to quit is the signal that an opportunity to excel is at hand.

— *Greg Quinn*

Never despair; but if you do, work on in despair.

— *Terence*

There will be times when you will feel alone and deserted, when you will feel weak and doubt yourself and wonder if you are stark raving mad, but if you endure and persevere, eventually you will arrive at your dream.

— *Les Brown*

April 9

The Power of Forgiveness
Forgiveness is the oil of relationships.
— *Josh McDowell*

God has forgiven you; you'd be wise to do the same.
— *Max Lucado*

Forgiveness is the key that unlocks the door of resentment and the handcuffs of hate. It is a power that breaks the chains of bitterness and the shackles of selfishness.
— *Corrie ten Boom*

Forgiveness without forgetting is not forgiveness at all – only an empty gesture. Forgiveness is the real thing only when we struggle and succeed in putting the hurt behind us. This makes us truly free of it so that it does not impede our love – much as a pebble in a shoe hurts the foot with each step taken.
— *Dr. Theodore Rubin*

April 10

The Power of Courage
Only those who dare to fail greatly can ever achieve greatly.
> — *Herodotus*

Courage is fear holding on a minute longer.
> — *General George Patton*

God grant me the courage not to give up what I think is right, even though I think it is hopeless.
> — *Admiral Chester Nimitz*

Courage is contagious. When a brave man takes a stand, the spines of others are stiffened.
> — *Billy Graham*

April 11

The Negative Committee
I have to remember to tell the negative committee that meets in my head to sit down and shut up.
— *Kathy Kendall*

The most handicapped person in the world is a negative thinker.
— *Heather Whitestone, Miss America 1994, who is deaf*

The more you let your mind dwell on negatives, of whatever type, the larger they grow and the greater the risk you will convert them into excuses.
— *Jack Nicklaus*

Maintain an attitude of unconditional self-worth, free from self-criticism. You can agree that it is cruel and unnecessary to tell someone else, "You are really stupid – what a klutz – you should give up – you keep making the same mistakes – you'll never be any good!" If you would never say those things to anyone else, why not pay yourself the same courtesy?
— *Dan Millman*

April 12

The Power of Prayer
A man who is intimate with God will never be intimidated by men.
— *Leonard Ravenhill*

You may ask me for anything in my name, and I will do it.
— *John 14:14*

I have found the greatest power in the world is the power of prayer.
— *Cecil B. DeMille*

So I say to you: Ask and it will be given to you; seek and you will find; knock and the door will be opened to you. For everyone who asks receives; he who seeks finds; and to him who knocks, the door will be opened.
— *Luke 11:9-10*

April 13

Adversity

The ultimate measure of a man is not where he stands in moments of comfort and convenience, but where he stands at times of challenge and controversy.
— *Martin Luther King, Jr.*

Once you are really challenged, you find something in yourself. Man doesn't know what he is capable of until he is asked.
— *Kofi Annan*

Do not give up when you find that you have to suffer greatly in order to get results. Never forget that the winners are the ones who can suffer best. It's the no-hopers who cannot suffer. The inability to suffer is almost always the real reason riders do not succeed in our sport. He who can suffer best has the best chance to get to the top.
— *Charles Ruys*

In the depth of winter, I finally learned that there was in me an invincible summer.
— *Albert Camus*

April 14

The Power of Laughter
A good laugh overcomes more difficulties and dissipates more dark clouds than any other one thing.
— *Laura Ingalls Wilder*

I believe in laughter. I think it is food for the soul.
— *Tommy Lasorda*

Against the assault of laughter nothing can stand.
— *Mark Twain*

Once you can laugh at your own weaknesses, you can move forward. Comedy breaks down walls. It opens up people, and you can fill up those openings with something positive.
— *Goldie Hawn*

April 15

Overcome Failure

Be of good cheer. Do not think of today's failures, but of the success that may come tomorrow.
— *Helen Keller*

To bear failure with courage is the best proof of character anyone can give. Do not let anyone see your mortification, but whatever you fancy people are saying about you, go on with your life as though nothing unpleasant has happened to you.
— *W. Somerset Maugham*

Perhaps only when human effort had done its best and failed, would God's power alone be free to work.
— *Corrie ten Boom*

I learned the lesson about not fearing failure from my dad because I've seen him fail and know what a great man he is. Losing a campaign does not mean losing your integrity, or losing your decency or losing his standing in my eyes or in the eyes of honorable people. We must take risks in order to succeed and if it doesn't work out for the moment, life itself will work out in the long run.
— *George W. Bush*

April 16

Receiving Criticism

So what if someone else thinks your dreams are dumb? What do they know? God hasn't called you to do what other people expect of you. He has called you to do something that is between you and Him alone.

— *Pat Williams*

He who listens to a life-giving rebuke will be at home among the wise.

— *Proverbs 15:31*

I remember when I was in college, people told me I couldn't play in the NBA. There's always somebody saying you can't do it, and those people have to be ignored.

— *Bill Cartwright*

Do not listen to those who say, "It is not done that way." Maybe it is not, but maybe you will.

— *Neil Simon*

April 17

Worry

When I've had a rough day, before I go to sleep I ask myself if there's anything more I can do right now. If there isn't, I sleep sound.
— *L.L. Colbert*

If only the people who worry about their liabilities would think about the riches they possess, they would stop worrying.
— *Dale Carnegie*

It is not only wrong to worry, it is infidelity, because worrying means that we do not think that God can look after the practical details of our lives.
— *Oswald Chambers*

It's not the cares of today, but the cares of tomorrow that weigh a man down. For the needs of today we have corresponding strength given. For the morrow we are told to trust. It is not ours yet.
— *George MacDonald*

April 18

God's Guidance

If any man desires to act according to the mind of God, light will come to him sooner or later.
— *Charles Haddon Spurgeon*

Whether you turn to the right or to the left, your ears will hear a voice behind you, saying, "This is the way; walk in it."
— *Isaiah 30:21*

He guides the humble in what is right and teaches them his way.
— *Psalm 25:9*

When God gives you direction, give Him all the time He needs to make you the kind of person that He can trust with that assignment. Do not assume that the moment He calls, you are ready.
— *Henry Blackaby*

April 19

Overcome Difficulties

Man's extremity is God's opportunity.
— *Thomas Adams*

A workable and effective way to meet and overcome difficulties is to take on someone else's problems. It is a strange fact, but you can often handle two difficulties – your own and somebody else's – better than you can handle your own alone. That truth is based on a subtle law of self-giving or outgoingness whereby you develop a self-strengthening in the process.
— *Norman Vincent Peale*

Nothing is worthwhile that is not hard. You do not improve your muscle by doing the easy thing; you improve it by doing the hard thing, and you get your zest by doing a thing that is difficult, not a thing that is easy.
— *Woodrow Wilson*

Don't overreact to current troubles; remember past accomplishments that help keep your confidence high.
— *Joe Torre*

April 20

Overcome Weaknesses

I feel no flattery when people speak of my voice. I'm simply grateful that I found a way to work around my stuttering.
— *James Earl Jones*

No matter how many times you aim to achieve victory over your passions, do not give up. Every effort weakens the power of passion and makes it easier to gain victory over it.
— *Leo Tolstoy*

Face your deficiencies and acknowledge them; but do not let them master you. Let them teach you patience, sweetness, insight.
— *Helen Keller*

When a man has no strength, if he leans on God, he becomes powerful.
— *D.L. Moody*

April 21

The Power of Commitment
When you get into a tight place and everything goes against you, until it seems as though you could not hold on a minute longer, never give up then, for that is just the place and time that the tide will turn.
— *Harriet Beecher Stowe*

It's important to keep trying to do what you think is right no matter how hard it is or how often you fail.
— *John Wooden*

Now if you are going to win any battle you have to do one thing. You have to make the mind run the body. The body will always give up. It is always tired morning, noon and night. But the body is never tired if the mind is not tired. When you were younger the mind could make you dance all night, and the body was never tired. You've always got to make the mind take over and keep going.
— *General George Patton*

As a young man I wrote for eight years without ever earning a nickel, which is a long apprenticeship, but in that time I learned a lot about my trade.
— *James Michener*

April 22

The Power of Faith

Stepping out in faith always brings clarification of God's plan.

— *Charles Swindoll*

Faith sings in your heart, no matter what assaults your soul.

— *Lester Sumrall*

Faith sees the invisible, believes the incredible and receives the impossible.

— *Corrie ten Boom*

When real faith grips you, you develop a mind-set that looks for the best in everything, refuses to give up, finds a way around (or through) every obstacle, and presses on to victory.

— *Norman Vincent Peale*

April 23

God Gives Us Power
All of God's greats have been weak men who did great exploits for God because they reckoned on His being faithful.
— *J. Hudson Taylor*

I can do everything through him who gives me strength.
— *Philippians 4:13*

When targeting problems, realize that what makes the Christian home different is not the absence of problems or conflict, but the presence of a problem solver within.
— *Howard Hendricks*

Jesus Christ never issues a call that we're incapable of responding to, but the timing of His call always seems too soon to us. We think we need more – more time, more money, more preparations, more qualifications, more . . . But He won't waste time by calling us into His purpose prematurely or by allowing us to linger beyond the timing He knows is best.
— *Jack Hayford*

April 24

Do the Impossible
Never let another person tell you that something cannot be done. God may have been waiting centuries for you to come along so that you could do the impossible for Him.

— *John Maxwell*

An extraordinary situation calls for extraordinary resolution. How many things have appeared impossible which, nevertheless, have been done by resolute men?

— *Napoléon Bonaparte*

God gets the greatest glory when we attack the greatest giants.

— *Rick Warren*

Don't listen to anyone who tells you that you can't do this or that. That's nonsense. Make up your mind, then have a go at everything. Never, never let them persuade you that things are too difficult or impossible.

— *Sir Douglas Bader*

April 25

When Bad Things Happen

I walked a mile with Sorrow
    And never a word said she;
    But, oh, the things I learned from her
    When Sorrow walked with me.

— *Robert Hamilton*

You will weep no more. How gracious he will be when you cry for help! As soon as he hears, he will answer you.

— *Isaiah 30:19*

He who sings drives away sorrow.

— *Anonymous*

No words can express how much the world owes to sorrow. Most of the Psalms were born in a wilderness. Most of the Epistles were written in a prison. Take comfort, afflicted Christian. When God is about to make pre-eminent use of a person, He puts them in the fire.

— *George MacDonald*

April 26

Great Potential

Continuous effort – not strength or intelligence – is the key to unlocking our potential.
— *Sir Winston Churchill*

Unless a man undertakes more than he possibly can do, he will never do all he can do.
— *Henry Drummond*

There is a giant asleep within every man. When that giant wakes, miracles happen.
— *Max Brand*

Within us all there are wells of thought and dynamos of energy which are not suspected until emergencies arise. Then oftentimes we find that it is comparatively simple to double or triple our former capacities and to amaze ourselves by the results achieved.
— *Thomas Watson*

April 27

Pressure

Pressure usually represents opportunity.
— *Jimmy Connors*

Pressure is neither good nor bad. You can convert pressure into negative tension and worry – or positive expectation and enthusiasm. It's a choice you make yourself.
— *Edge Keynote*

You never will be the person you can be if pressure, tension and discipline are taken out of your life.
— *James Bilkey*

Since stress is the body's way of dealing with threats, a simple way to de-stress is to use your body's response to good things to your advantage. A few moments spent thinking how lucky you are to be alive or how grateful you are to be loved or how in awe you are of nature's beauty all send a chemical message that life is good throughout your body.
— *Frederic Luskin*

April 28

Benefit from Failure
Mistakes are the portals of discovery.
— *James Joyce*

Defeat supplants vanity and arrogance with humility, paving the way for more harmonious relationships.
— *Napoleon Hill*

We learn wisdom from failure much more than from success; we often discover what will do, by finding out what will not do; and probably he who never made a mistake never made a discovery.
— *Samuel Smiles*

Where you stumble and fall, there you discover gold.
— *Joseph Campbell*

April 29

Strong Character

I can honestly say that I was never affected by the question of the success of a task. If I felt it was the right thing to do, I was for it regardless of the possible outcome.

— *Golda Meir*

The way to fame goes through the palaces, the way to happiness goes through the markets, the way to virtue goes through the deserts.

— *Chinese proverb*

It's not hard to make decisions when you know what your values are.

— *Roy Disney*

My obligation is to do the right thing. The rest is in God's hands.

— *Martin Luther King, Jr.*

April 30

The Adversity Advantage

Every experience, however bitter, has its lesson, and to focus one's attention on the lesson helps one overcome the bitterness.

— *Edward Griggs*

Sometimes adverse circumstances are testing devices, providing means by which you may be promoted from a given task to a greater one.

— *Napoleon Hill*

Adversity has made many a man great who, had he remained prosperous, would only have been rich.

— *Maurice Switzer*

I have often thought it would be a blessing if each human being were stricken blind and deaf for a few days during his early adult life. Darkness would make him more appreciative of sight; silence would teach him the joys of sound.

— *Helen Keller*

May 1

Fulfill Your Purpose

If a man does not keep pace with his companions, perhaps it is because he hears a different drummer. Let him step to the music he hears, however measured or far away.

— *Henry David Thoreau*

Bringing enjoyment to God, living for His pleasure, is the first purpose of your life. When you fully understand this truth, you will never again have a problem with feeling insignificant.

— *Rick Warren*

You don't need to be president of the company to be successful. You just have to be faithful to your purpose and please God by so doing.

— *John Stanko*

If a man is called to be a streetsweeper, he should sweep streets even as Michelangelo painted, or Beethoven composed music or Shakespeare wrote poetry. He should sweep streets so well that all the hosts of heaven and earth will pause to say, here lived a great streetsweeper who did his job well.

— *Martin Luther King, Jr.*

May 2

Renewal

We should all learn to have fun right now, in the present moment, to take whatever joy life has to offer.
— *Pat Williams*

Reading enables me to escape my life and the demands of others. It allows my soul the chance to throw open a window and ventilate my life with the fresh experiences of some enjoyable character with a life very different from my own.
— *T.D. Jakes*

Lie on your back and look at the stars.
— *H. Jackson Brown, Jr.*

When you feel tired, frazzled, stressed or overwhelmed, it's important to stop and refresh your spirit and nurture your body. During a *time-out*, you'll rekindle your spirit and perhaps even receive some important insights.
— *Joan Lunden*

May 3

Overcome Fear

Don't let the sensation of fear convince you that you're too weak to have courage. Fear is the opportunity for courage, not proof of cowardice.
— *John McCain*

Don't be afraid to take a big step. You can't cross a chasm in two small steps.
— *David George*

With any fear, you have to face it head-on. It's your only way to progress. Your biggest fears contain your biggest opportunities to develop as a human being.
— *Annika Sorenstam*

Do not listen to yourself when the little voice of fear inside of you rears its ugly head and says, "They are all smarter than you out there. They are more talented, they are taller, blonder, prettier, luckier and have connections. They have a cousin who took out Meryl Streep's baby-sitter." Give credence at all to that voice, and your worst fears will surely come true.
— *Neil Simon*

May 4

Resolve Conflict
The aim of an argument or discussion should not be victory, but progress.
— *Joseph Joubert*

You don't have to win every argument. Agree to disagree.
— *Reginna Brett*

He has power who can keep silent in an argument, even though he is right.
— *Leo Tolstoy*

You will never get into trouble by admitting that you may be wrong. That will stop all argument and inspire your opponent to be just as fair and open and broad-minded as you are. It will make him want to admit that he, too, may be wrong.
— *Dale Carnegie*

May 5

Commitment

I could accept failure, but I could never accept quitting.
— *Betsy Cullen, on winning her first tournament after her eighth year on tour*

Patience and perseverance have a magical effect before which difficulties disappear and obstacles vanish.
— *John Quincy Adams*

The sorriest man is the man who knows he gave up before he exhausted his efforts because he must look back and wonder, "What if?"
— *Gary Player*

One thing I've noticed in all my years of coaching is that the most successful athletes, the most successful people in all walks of life, in fact, have one thing in common – they persist. They refuse to let anyone tell them their dreams can't come true. They never waver in their belief in themselves. They refuse to be denied.
— *Rick Pitino*

May 6

God's Will

Even when His will doesn't make sense from your human perspective, your obedience will reveal that His will was right.

— *Henry Blackaby*

The center of God's will is our only safety.

— *Betsie ten Boom*

Outside the will of God, there's nothing I want, and in the will of God there's nothing I fear.

— *A.W. Tozer*

God may be leading you somewhere that doesn't make much sense. I want to encourage you: Don't try to make sense out of it, just go. If God leads you to stay in a difficult situation and you have peace that you are to stay, don't analyze it, stay. Do your part. Do what He tells you to do, for His promises often hinge on obedience.

— *Charles Swindoll*

May 7

Start Where You Are
Every successful man I have heard of has done the best he could with conditions as he found them, and not waited until the next year for better.
— *Edgar Howe*

Get rid of *if only* thinking. You can achieve excellence as you are.
— *Pat Williams*

Use what talents you have; the woods would have little music if no birds sang their song except those who sang best.
— *Oliver Wilson*

If you wait for perfect conditions, you will never get anything done . . . . keep on sowing your seed, for you never know which will grow – perhaps it all will.
— *Ecclesiastes 11:4-6 (TLB)*

May 8

Help from Others

If you isolate your problem from others, your chances of solving it are thin. Problems require wisdom, and wisdom requires perspective. Other people provide that perspective.
— *Bill Russell*

The smartest thing I ever said was, "Help Me!"
— *Anonymous*

Two are better than one, because they have a good return for their work: If one falls down, his friend can help him up.
— *Ecclesiastes 4:9-10*

Discover someone to help shoulder your misfortunes. Then you will never be alone. Neither fate, nor the crowd, so readily attacks two.
— *Baltasar Gracián*

May 9

Faith

Don't doubt your faith, doubt your doubts for they are unreliable.

— *F.F. Bosworth*

Faith opens the door of God's promise for you; and patience keeps it open until that promise is fulfilled.

— *Kenneth Copeland*

The human spirit, once stretched by an adventure of faith, will never return to its original size.

— *Anonymous*

In my life, I've discovered two kinds of faith – a delivering faith and a sustaining faith. Delivering faith is when God instantly turns your situation around. When that happens, it's great. But I believe it takes a greater faith and a deeper walk with God to have that sustaining faith.

— *Joel Osteen*

May 10

Failure
My dad used to repeat a line of Samuel Beckett's so often that I had it pinned on my wall at home: "Keep on failing. Only this time fail better."
— *Joely Richarson*

Determination conquers every failure.
— *Pat Riley*

You will never really be sure you have aimed high enough until you have suffered a failure.
— *Robert Schuller*

"Success is not about winning or losing," my dad told me on more than one occasion, when I felt I had been treated unfairly, or my team hadn't been victorious, or another kid in class had gotten a higher grade than I had. "Your real success in life comes from adjusting," he'd say. "How well you adjust, how quickly you adjust and how sensitively you adjust will make all the difference at the end of the day."
— *Peter Greenberg*

May 11

The Power of Positive Thinking

The pessimist sees difficulty in every opportunity. The optimist sees opportunity in every difficulty.
— *Sir Winston Churchill*

The enemy is in front of us, behind us, to the left of us and to the right of us. They can't escape us this time!
— *Lewis Puller, marine lieutenant*

Optimism enables a man to hold his head high, to claim the future for himself and not abandon it to his enemy.

— *Dietrich Bonhoeffer*

The next time you try that task, don't think about the time you faltered. Think about all of the times in which you have excelled. That's a path back to success.

— *Derek Jeter*

❧ May 12

The Importance of Prayer
He who moves mountains must make prayer a life habit.
— *Gordon Lindsay*

Prayer is an armor – do not go into your day without it.
— *Anonymous*

Each morning I will look to you in heaven and lay my requests before you, praying earnestly.
— *Psalm 5:3 (TLB)*

We kneel, how weak! We rise, how full of power!
— *Richard Trench*

May 13

Overcome Difficulties

Amid the greatest difficulties of my administration, when I could not see any other resort, I would place my whole reliance in God, knowing that all would go well and that He would decide for the right.
— *Abraham Lincoln*

The more difficult a victory, the greater the happiness in winning.
— *Pelé*

One reason we get so stressed when something goes wrong is that we focus only on what has gone wrong. We wish it hadn't happened and mumble about our rotten luck. Instead, try reframing a problem situation to see if there is any possible good in it.
— *Dr. Suzanne Zoglio*

They gave Him a manger for a cradle, a carpenter's bench for a pulpit, thorns for a crown and a cross for a throne. He took them and made them the very glory of His career.
— *W.E. Orchard*

May 14

Success
The worst bankrupt is the man who has lost his enthusiasm. Let a man lose everything in the world but his enthusiasm and he will come through again to success.
— *H.W. Arnold*

Anything worth anything takes some doing, takes sacrifice. To seize life and live fully invites the potential for pain and disappointment. But that's the risk you take so that you can stand proud knowing you've lived, you've played, while countless others never got off the bench.
— *Margaret Spellings*

In order to succeed greatly, you have to sacrifice greatly. Nobody ever said it would be easy.
— *Mike Pruitt*

Define success in terms of how well you honor your commitment to the process.
— *Dr. Bob Rotella*

May 15

Overcome Temptation

The Bible teaches us in times of temptation there is one command. Flee! Get away from it, for every struggle against lust using only one's own strength is doomed to failure.

— *Dietrich Bonhoeffer*

No one can ask honestly or happily to be delivered from temptation unless he has honestly and firmly determined to do the best he can to keep out of it.

— *John Ruskin*

Resist the devil, and he will flee from you.

— *James 4:7*

No temptation has seized you except what is common to man. And God is faithful; he will not let you be tempted beyond what you can bear. But when you are tempted, he will also provide a way out so that you can stand up under it.

— *1 Corinthians 10:13*

May 16

Today Is the Day
I will work when failures seek rest. I will act now for now is all I have. Tomorrow is the day reserved for the labor of the lazy. I am not lazy. Tomorrow is the day when the failure will succeed. I am not a failure. I will act now. Success will not wait.

— Og Mandino

Today is mine. Tomorrow is none of my business. If I peer anxiously into the fog of the future, I will strain my spiritual eyes so that I will not see clearly what is required of me now.

— Elisabeth Elliot

We can learn from past failures and mistakes, but we shouldn't get stuck there. We can keep future goals in mind, but we shouldn't get stuck there, either. The only way to reach our potential is to focus on what we must do now – this moment, this day – to perform effectively and win.

— Joe Torre

Burn the candles, use the nice sheets, wear the fancy lingerie. Don't save it for a special occasion. Today is special.

— Reginna Brett

May 17

God Will Provide

Have courage for the great sorrows of life and patience for the small ones. And when you have laboriously accomplished your daily task, go to sleep in peace. God is awake.

— *Victor Hugo*

None of us can see the future, but we can know for sure that whenever we get there, God will have been there ahead of us. And as long as He's there, what do we have to fear?

— *Pat Williams*

I was young and now I am old, yet I have never seen the righteous forsaken or their children begging bread.

— *Psalm 37:25*

Where can I go from your Spirit? Where can I flee from your presence? If I go up to the heavens, you are there; if I make my bed in the depths, you are there. If I rise on the wings of the dawn, if I settle on the far side of the sea, even there your hand will guide me, your right hand will hold me fast.

— *Psalm 139:7-10*

May 18

The Power of Commitment
Most of the important things in the world have been accomplished by people who have kept on trying when there seemed to be no hope at all.

— *Dale Carnegie*

It took me twelve years to become an overnight sensation.

— *Toby Harrah*

God has a way for us to do everything He places in our heart. He does not put dreams and visions in us to frustrate us. We must keep our confidence all the way through to the end, not just for a little bit and then when it looks like the mountain is too big, give up.

— *Joyce Meyer*

Through perseverance many people win success out of what seemed destined to be certain failure.

— *Benjamin Disraeli*

May 19

Adversity

Obstacles don't have to stop you. If you run into a wall, don't turn around and give up. Figure out how to climb it, go through it or work around it.

— *Michael Jordan*

It's up to us how we respond to adversity. We can go into a blue funk, give up, quit, or, as Billy Graham taught me to do, we can say, "Thank you, God, for giving me this challenge. I'll show you what I'm made of," and respond with courage, enthusiasm and even joy.

— *Gary Player*

Frame every so-called disaster with these words: "In five years, will this matter?"

— *Reginna Brett*

Not only are we comforted in our trials, but our trials can equip us to comfort others.

— *Billy Graham*

May 20

The Power of Music

Music washes away from the soul the dust of every-day life.

— *Berthold Auerbach*

When life feels like a grind, change the rhythm. Put on some toe-tapping music and get moving. Hum, whistle along or sing out loud. It's difficult to stay down when the joy of music surrounds you.

— *Dr. Suzanne Zoglio*

Songs are funny things. They can slip across borders. Proliferate in prisons. Penetrate hard shells. I always believed that the right song at the right moment could change history.

— *Pete Seeger*

Take a music bath once or twice a week for a few seasons. You will find that it is to the soul what the water bath is to the body.

— *Oliver Wendell Holmes*

May 21

Become Wise

Who is wise? He that learns from everyone.
— *Benjamin Franklin*

If any of you lacks wisdom, he should ask God, who gives generously to all without finding fault, and it will be given to him.
— *James 1:5*

Knowledge is horizontal; wisdom is vertical and comes from above.
— *Billy Graham*

Do you know what I've discovered about the Lord? He doesn't give wisdom on credit. He doesn't advance you a bundle of insight. Do you know when He gives us words and wisdom and insight? Right when we need them.
— *Charles Swindoll*

May 22

Greatness

Like an ant carrying a morsel of bread to his dwelling place, greatness is often dragged by persons who seem too small.

— *T.D. Jakes*

God does not always choose great people to accomplish what He wishes, but He chooses a person who is wholly yielded to Him.

— *Henrietta C. Mears*

The people we admire are ordinary people that have been able to accomplish some extraordinary things. The things that make them extraordinary are things that we all possess.

— *Rolf Benirschke*

God is looking not for great people but for people who will dare to prove the greatness of their God.

— *L.B. Cowman*

May 23

Benefit from Failure

The better a man is, the more mistakes he will make, for the more new things he will try. I would never promote into a top-level job a man who was not making mistakes, otherwise he is sure to be mediocre.
— *Peter Drucker*

Failure is the opportunity to begin again more intelligently.
— *Henry Ford*

I have not failed. I've just found 10,000 ways that don't work.
— *Thomas Edison*

It is only because of problems that we grow mentally and spiritually.
— *M. Scott Peck*

May 24

Risks

There is no guarantee of success in anything you want to accomplish. In fact, if you seek the guarantee of success, you will never succeed. If you're not willing to take risks or to fail, you cannot succeed.
— *Benjamin Netanyahu*

There are hazards in everything one does; but there are greater hazards in doing nothing.
— *Shirley Williams*

I postpone death by living, by suffering, by error, by mistaking, by giving, by losing.
— *Anaïs Nin*

When I began to fear that I would fall flat on my face (and possibly with disastrous results) on Mount Rainier, I responded to those doubts by reminding myself that it is okay to risk failure. I knew that I would have a much easier time living with failure than with knowing I had never tried at all.
— *Pat Williams*

May 25

When God Is Silent

The kind of faith God values seems to develop best when everything fuzzes over, when God stays silent, when the fog rolls in.

— *Philip Yancey*

If God chooses to remain silent, faith is content.
— *Ruth Bell Graham*

We often equate faith with great deeds and incredible results in the face of overwhelming odds. But I'll take the faith that is tested day after day after day with nothing to show for it but a firm belief in the ultimate goodness of God.

— *Paul Johnson*

The school of faith teaches us to trust God to solve our problems, and then, for a graduate course, it teaches us to trust God when He chooses not to solve our problems.

— *Stephen Goard*

May 26

The Adversity Advantage
Comfort and prosperity have never enriched the world as much as adversity. Out of pain and problems have come the sweetest songs, the most touching poems, the most gripping stories and inspiring lives.

— *Billy Graham*

The greater the difficulty, the more glory in surmounting it.

— *Epicurus*

Adversity puts things in perspective. If you let it, it can help you focus on things that really count in your life. You can free yourself from trivialities and concentrate on what's really important.

— *Pat Williams*

The sermon of your life in tough times ministers to people more powerfully than the most eloquent speaker.

— *Bill Bright*

May 27

God Gives Us Power
God's strength behind you, His concern for you, His love within you and His arms beneath you are more than sufficient for the job ahead of you.
— *William Ward*

I don't think I could have been so successful if I didn't have faith in a higher being. There are times when I get so tired. But with God, I know something bigger is driving me, I can do anything.
— *Claire Prymus*

My grace is sufficient for you, for my power is made perfect in weakness.
— *2 Corinthians 12:9*

God will never call you to do something unless He also provides the means for you to have the energy and resources to accomplish His task. You may have to work hard, but God never requires that you have a nervous, emotional or physical breakdown in the process.
— *Charles Stanley*

May 28

Your Self-image

I was brought up to believe that how I saw myself was more important than how others saw me.
— *Anwar El-Sadat*

Your self-image is extremely important. It plays a major role in determining your place in life. You need to work on seeing yourself achieving great things.
— *Dr. Bob Rotella*

What others say of me matters little; what I myself say and do matters much.
— *Elbert Hubbard*

We were created in God's image, and God is no weakling.
— *Charles Atlas*

May 29

Serve Others

The infectiously joyous men and women are those who forget themselves in thinking about others and serving others.
— *Robert McCracken*

When you make the stew and someone else gets the strokes, remember your role: to serve and to give.
— *Charles Swindoll*

Try to forget yourself in the service of others. For when we think too much of ourselves and our own interests, we easily become despondent. But when we work for others, our efforts return to bless us.
— *Sidney Powell*

The roots of happiness grow deepest in the soil of service.
— *Anonymous*

May 30

Receiving Criticism
The small man flies into a rage over the slightest criticism, but the wise man is eager to learn from those who censure and reprove him.
— *Dale Carnegie*

Many times during auditions, I was told that I couldn't carry a note with a bucket, and that I sure couldn't play the piano.
— *Ray Charles*

Every truth passes through three stages before it is recognized. In the first it is ridiculed, in the second it is opposed, in the third it is regarded as self-evident.
— *Arthur Schopenhauer*

I wasn't supposed to reach my dream of being a baseball player. If I had listened to all those people who muttered, "Good luck, kid," when they heard me say when I was young that I wanted to be a Yankee, I would have given up a long time ago.
— *Derek Jeter*

May 31

When Bad Things Happen

Troubles are often the tools by which God fashions us for better things.
— *Henry Ward Beecher*

Those held in highest esteem by most people are those who master a hard lot with their head held high.
— *Viktor Frankl*

Trouble is a part of life, and if you don't share it, you don't give the person who loves you a chance to love you enough.
— *Dinah Shore*

When will we ever learn that there are no hopeless situations, only people who have grown hopeless about them? What appears as an unsolvable problem to us is actually a rather exhilarating challenge. People who inspire others are those who see invisible bridges at the end of dead-end streets.
— *Charles Swindoll*

June 1

The Power of Commitment

Effort only fully releases its reward after a person refuses to quit.
— *Napoleon Hill*

The longest voyages make the richest returns.
— *Matthew Henry*

Great works are performed not by strength, but perseverance.
— *Samuel Johnson*

There are but two roads that lead to an important goal and to the doing of great things: strength and perseverance. Strength is the lot of but a few privileged men; but austere perseverance, harsh and continuous, may be employed by the smallest of us and rarely fails of its purpose, for its silent power grows irresistibly greater with time.
— *Johann von Goethe*

❧ June 2

Worry
Life follows the 95/5 rule. Ninety-five percent of what we worry about will never happen. And 95 percent of the time, if it does happen, the anticipation has been far worse than the reality.
— *Roger Crawford*

Work doesn't make a person tired, worry does. It saps your energy and attacks your dreams. It tries to make you believe you can't succeed when success is almost within your grasp. Win over worry, and you'll find that victory is at hand.
— *John Maxwell*

All worry is caused by calculating without God.
— *Oswald Chambers*

Every morning I spend fifteen minutes filling my mind full of God, so there's no room left for worry thoughts.
— *Howard Christy*

June 3

The Power of Change
Change is what keeps us fresh and innovative. Change is what keeps us from getting stale and stuck in a rut. Change is what keeps us young.
— *Rick Pitino*

One must never lose time in vainly regretting the past or in complaining against the changes which cause us discomfort, for change is the essence of life.
— *Anatole France*

Change provides the opportunity for innovation. It gives you the chance to demonstrate your creativity.
— *Keshavan Nair*

Welcome change as a friend; try to visualize new possibilities and the blessings they are bound to bring to you. If you stay interested in everything around you – in new ways of life, new people, new places and ideas – you'll stay young, no matter what your age. Never stop learning and never stop growing. This is the key to a rich and fascinating life.
— *Alexander De Seversky*

June 4

Overcome Failure
When I was young, I observed that nine out of every ten things I did were failures, so I did ten times more work.
— *George Bernard Shaw*

Always imitate the behavior of the winners when you lose.
— *George Meredith*

We fail more often than we succeed. You can't let those failures get to you, because they will erode your confidence and chip away at your psyche.
— *Tiger Woods*

Sports taught me that I can make a mistake one minute, let it go, and be brilliant the next.
— *Lynn Sherr*

June 5

The Power of Humor

Humor is the best therapy.
— *Norman Cousins*

Fear promotes failure. Humor controls fear.
— *Tim McCarver*

Humor is a social lubricant that helps us get over some of the bad spots.
— *Steve Allen*

Humor acts as a buffer against stress, an antidote to paralyzing perfectionism and a way to widen your perspective. It wards off depression and contributes to good health.
— *Roger Crawford*

June 6

Career Development
If the career you have chosen has some unexpected inconvenience, console yourself by reflecting that no career is without them.
— *Jane Fonda*

Never admit at work that you're tired, angry or bored.
— *H. Jackson Brown, Jr.*

If you have a job without aggravations, you don't have a job.
— *Malcolm Forbes*

If you are having trouble pursuing your passion, you can still find real happiness by putting passion into your current pursuits. Each of us can find our calling where we are, right now, if we only begin to see the higher purpose to our task. The farmer provides nourishment, the builder gives shelter, the office worker offers assistance and solves problems for customers and fellow workers.
— *Thomas Kinkade*

June 7

Overcome Difficulties

Few destinations have one point of access. The same is true of your vision. If your initial approach is blocked, look for alternatives.

— *Andy Stanley*

We must never despair; our situation has been compromising before, and it has changed for the better; so I trust it will again.

— *George Washington*

It is not always by plugging away at a difficulty and sticking to it that one overcomes it; often it is by working on the one next to it. Some things and some people have to be approached obliquely, at an angle.

— *André Gide*

I am a woman who came from the cotton fields of the South. From there I was promoted to the washtub. From there I was promoted to the cook kitchen. And from there I promoted myself into the business of manufacturing hair products.

— *C.J. Walker*

June 8

Enjoy Beauty

Steeping my life in beauty brings color to my days and a song to my heart.

— *Thomas Kinkade*

Many eyes go through the meadow, but few see the flowers in it.

— *Ralph Waldo Emerson*

Always have something beautiful in sight, even if it's just a daisy in a jelly glass.

— *H. Jackson Brown, Jr.*

Why is beauty so important? Because we derive energy and motivation from beautiful sights, beautiful sounds, beautiful words and ideas, and beautiful environments. Beauty is food for the soul, balm to the spirit, inspiration for anything worthwhile we do with our lives.

— *Thomas Kinkade*

June 9

Great Decisions

Those who can tolerate ambiguity and make decisions in the face of uncertainty will rise to the top.
— *Helen Peters*

Make major decisions in a cemetery.
— *Max Lucado*

Seldom do you enjoy the luxury of making decisions that are based on enough evidence to absolutely silence all skepticism.
— *Bill Hybels*

If you wait to make an important decision until all the information that you might want is in, you will never make it in time. Depending on the risks, on what the stakes are, you have to settle for 75, 70 or 65 percent of the information that you need, because the time and the cost of getting, say, the last 25 percent are not commensurate with what you might gain by deferring the decision.
— *Harold Geneen*

June 10

A Good Attitude

As soon as you believe it can be done, a great psychological barrier is broken and you begin to work toward higher goals.

— *Byron Nelson*

Our attitude toward things is likely to be more important than the things themselves.

— *A.W. Tozer*

If I always believe in myself, regardless of what anyone else feels, and I'm willing to work hard, then I can achieve anything I want.

— *Gail Devers*

If you want to change attitudes, start with a change in behavior. In other words, begin to act the part, as well as you can, of the person you would rather be, the person you most want to become. Gradually, the old, fearful person will fade away.

— *William Glasser*

June 11

Prayer

We must not conceive of prayer as an overcoming of God's reluctance, but as a laying hold of His highest willingness.

— *Richard Trench*

Prayer must be filled with faith, uttered with boldness, offered in obedience and overflowing with praise and confidence.

— *Jack Hayford*

Groanings which cannot be uttered are often prayers which cannot be refused.

— *Charles Haddon Spurgeon*

There are four ways God answers prayer: No, not yet; No, I love you too much; Yes, I thought you'd never ask; Yes, and here's more.

— *Anne Lewis*

June 12

Overcome Adversity

Laugh a lot. A good sense of humor cures almost all of life's ills.

— *H. Jackson Brown, Jr.*

Turmoil, difficulty, persecution and hardship are not essential indicators of being out of God's will. On the contrary, there are times those things mean you are, in fact, in the nucleus of His plan.

— *Charles Swindoll*

Expect trouble as an inevitable part of life, and when it comes, hold your head high, look it squarely in the eye and say, "I will be bigger than you. You cannot defeat me." Then repeat to yourself the most comforting of all words, "This too shall pass."

— *Ann Landers*

The test of intelligence is not how much we know how to do, but how we behave when we don't know what to do. Similarly, any situation, any activity, that puts before us real problems that we have to solve for ourselves, problems for which there are no answers in any book, sharpens our intelligence.

— *John Holt*

June 13

The Power of Patience
Slow growing trees bear better fruit.
— *Jean Moliére*

Teach us, O Lord, the disciplines of patience, for we find that to wait is often harder than to work.
— *Peter Marshall*

When we read of the great Biblical leaders, we see that it was not uncommon for God to ask them to wait, not just a day or two, but for years, until God was ready for them to act.
— *Gloria Gaither*

The two most powerful warriors are patience and time.
— *Leo Tolstoy*

June 14

The Power of Faith

Worry and anxiety are sand in the machinery of life; faith is the oil.

— *E. Stanley Jones*

Faith hears the inaudible, sees the invisible, believes the incredible and receives the impossible.

— *Anonymous*

If you have faith as small as a mustard seed, you can say to this mountain, "Move from here to there" and it will move. Nothing will be impossible for you.

— *Matthew 17:20*

If you are moving in the energy of the flesh, you're doomed to fail. But when you trust the Lord God to give you the next step, when you wait in humility upon Him, He will open the doors or close them, and you'll get to rest and relax until He says, "Go."

— *Charles Swindoll*

June 15

The Power of Goals

You must have long-range goals to keep you from being frustrated by short-range failures.
— *Charles Noble*

If I fall a little bit short, then I'm still further ahead than if I hadn't reached at all.
— *Don Shula*

Goals help you overcome short-term problems.
— *Hannah More*

Courage is sustained by calling up anew the vision of the goal.
— *A.G. Sertillanges*

June 16

Build Courage
Courage is not the absence of fear, but rather the judgment that something else is more important than fear.
— *Ambrose Redmoon*

We must constantly build dikes of courage to hold back the flood of fear.
— *Martin Luther King, Jr.*

Never ask for victory, ask only for courage. For if you endure the struggle, you bring honor to yourself. But more important, you bring honor to us all.
— *Bill Mallon*

You gain strength, courage and confidence by every experience in which you really stop to look fear in the face. You are able to say to yourself, "I lived through this horror. I can take the next thing that comes along."
— *Eleanor Roosevelt*

June 17

Benefit from Failure

The most successful men have used seeming failures as stepping stones to better things.

— *Grenville Kleiser*

Some of my fondest memories in sport were a result of failure, injuries, setbacks or mistakes. I learned far more about myself and gained more character in those difficult times than I ever did when success came easily.

— *Peter Vidmar*

Success is 99 percent failure.

— *Soichire Honda*

People look at things closer when they lose than when they win. At least, that's what I found myself doing. Sometimes when you win, there's stuff under the couch and rug that you ignore. But when you suffer a real setback, you want to know all the reasons why – so that it will never happen again.

— *Mike Krzyzewski*

June 18

The Adversity Advantage
The most gifted members of the human species are at their creative best when they cannot have their way.
— *Eric Hoffer*

Adversity causes some men to break, others to break records.
— *William Ward*

It's a good thing to have all the props pulled out from under us occasionally. It gives us some sense of what is rock under our feet, and what is sand.
— *Madeleine L'Engle*

Circumstances may appear to wreck our lives and God's plans, but God is not helpless among the ruins. Our broken lives are not lost or useless. God comes in and takes the calamity and uses it victoriously, working out His wonderful plan of love.
— *Eric Liddell*

June 19

Financial Freedom

By borrowing, many people get ahead of God and wind up doing things He never intended them to do.
— *Ron Blue*

More money is not the answer; more discipline is. Until you decide to live on what you already make, more money will not help.
— *Larry Burkett*

Under budgetary pressure (arbitrary or not) it is truly remarkable how many options one discovers one can do without.
— *James Schlesinger*

Without frugality few can become rich, and with it few would become poor.
— *Samuel Johnson*

June 20

The Super Glue of Life

An apology is the super glue of life. It can repair almost anything.

— *Lynn Johnston*

Apologize immediately when you lose your temper, especially to children.

— *H. Jackson Brown, Jr.*

By admitting your mistakes, your inherent message is that you're trying to be conciliatory, that you really do want to correct the misunderstanding. Doing this immediately takes the other person off the defensive and enables that person to be more willing to own up to his or her mistakes.

— *Rick Pitino*

Be the first to say sorry. Saying sorry has many benefits, even if it does stick in your throat a little. Not only does it give you the moral advantage, but it also diffuses tension, gets rid of bad feelings and clears the air. Chances are that if you say sorry first, they will probably be humbled into apologizing also.

— *Richard Templar*

June 21

God's Guidance

We do not understand the intricate pattern of the stars in their courses, but we know that He who created them does, and that just as surely as He guides them, He is charting a safe course for us.

— *Billy Graham*

When we have asked God to guide us, we have to accept by faith the fact that He is doing so. This means that when He closes a door in our faces, then we do well not to try to crash that door.

— *Catherine Marshall*

Faith accepts quiet guidance. Only unbelief demands a miracle.

— *Anonymous*

Trust in the Lord with all your heart and lean not on your own understanding; in all your ways acknowledge him, and he will make your paths straight.

— *Proverbs 3:5-6*

June 22

Benefits of Exercise

When our minds race so rapidly that we don't know which way is up, it often helps to get physical. It may seem ironic, but it works. As you focus your energy on a physical task, the traffic in your mind will begin to thin out.

— *Dr. Suzanne Zoglio*

Exercise can be a tremendous mental and physical stimulant, clearing away sluggishness. It also teaches you persistence and concentration.

— *Napoleon Hill*

Exercise and physical fitness can act as buffers against stress.

— *Michael Sacks*

A vigorous five-mile walk will do more good for an unhappy but otherwise healthy adult than all the medicine and psychology in the world.

— *Paul White*

June 23

Leisure

I ran away from a thousand things waiting to be done and stole a little visit with a friend.
— *Laura Ingalls Wilder*

The moment one gives close attention to anything, even a blade of grass, it becomes a mysterious, awesome, indescribably magnificent world in itself.
— *Henry Miller*

If you would be free from nervous tension and live a healthier life, widen your interests, broaden yourself. There is a rich world around you in books, paintings, music, sports and most important, people.
— *Norman Vincent Peale*

When the spirits are low, when the day appears dark, when work becomes monotonous, when hope hardly seems worth having, just mount a bicycle and go out for a spin down the road, without thought on anything but the ride you are taking.
— *Sir Arthur Conan Doyle*

June 24

Start Where You Are
Now is no time to think of what you do not have. Think of what you can do with what there is.
— *Ernest Hemingway*

The question for each man is not what he would do if he had the means, time, influence and educational advantages, but what he will do with the things he has.
— *Frank Hamilton*

It is the greatest of all mistakes to do nothing because you can only do a little. Do what you can.
— *Sydney Smith*

Experience has taught me that if I focus predominantly on what I do not have, I am very seldom productive. More often than not, I am frustrated and discouraged. But if I focus only on what I have to work with, I start finding new solutions to old problems.
— *Art Berg*

June 25

Overcome Weaknesses

Demosthenes overcame his inarticulate and stammering pronunciation by speaking with pebbles in his mouth; his voice he disciplined by reciting speeches or verses when he was out of breath, while running or going up steep places.

— *Plutarch*

We must identify our weaknesses and allow a certain amount of time in our daily routine to turn those weaknesses into future strengths.

— *Rick Pitino*

What it comes down to is that anybody can win with the best horse. What makes you good is if you can take the second- or third-best horse and win.

— *Vicky Aragon*

Knowing that we are hopelessly weak is the first step toward receiving God's gift of might and strength.

— *Marva Dawn*

June 26

God Gives Us Power
If the Lord calls you, He will equip you for the task He wants you to fulfill.
— *Warren Wiersbe*

You're not alone. God will fight for you. And you can go ahead in spite of any fears you might have to take the new ground God is giving you.
— *Bruce Wilkinson*

We have this treasure in jars of clay to show that this all-surpassing power is from God and not from us.
— *2 Corinthians 4:7*

When times are good, it's easy for us to be on the up and up, easy to be the people we say we're supposed to be. But when times are hard, that's when your true character and your faith are tested. I just want to pass all those tests. When I focus on Jesus and don't rely on my strength, I'm able to do that.
— *Marques Tuiasosopo*

June 27

Be a Good Friend

The friend who holds your hand and says the wrong thing is made of dearer stuff than the one who stays away.

— *Barbara Kingsolver*

Really good people are few and far between – don't let them go because of dumb mistakes or misunderstandings. The best friendships allow for a little flakiness.

— *Mindy Morgenstern*

Relationships don't thrive because the guilty are punished but because the innocent are merciful.

— *Max Lucado*

Make allowances for your friends' imperfections as readily as you do for your own.

— *H. Jackson Brown, Jr.*

June 28

The Power of Commitment

Bear in mind, if you are going to amount to anything, that your success does not depend upon the brilliancy and the passion with which you take hold, but upon the bull-doggedness with which you hang on after you have taken hold.

— *A.B. Meldrum*

My golf is woeful, but I will never surrender.

— *Bing Crosby*

As you know, we consider blessed those who have persevered. You have heard of Job's perseverance and have seen what the Lord finally brought about. The Lord is full of compassion and mercy.

— *James 5:11*

Constant effort and frequent mistakes are the stepping-stones of genius.

— *Elbert Hubbard*

June 29

Admit Mistakes

Conceal a flaw, and the world will imagine the worst.
— *Marcus Martial*

Confident leaders freely admit their own mistakes. And by doing it publicly, they set an example for others to take responsibility.
— *Bill Parcells*

A man should never be ashamed to admit he was wrong, which is but saying that he is wiser today than he was yesterday.
— *Alexander Pope*

Admit when you're wrong. When I'm courageous enough to admit I'm wrong or I've made a mistake, I'm amazed at the generosity of the person on the receiving end. This increases trust, elevates credibility and strengthens the relationship.
— *Vickie Milazzo*

June 30

Adversity
If you break your neck, if you have nothing to eat, if your house is on fire – then you got a problem. Everything else is inconvenience.
— *Robert Fulgham*

It's not so much what you accomplish in life that really matters, but what you overcome that proves who you are, what you are and whether you are a champion.
— *Johnny Miller*

Knowing how to benefit from failure is the key to success, and if your kids see you benefiting in your life on a daily basis and growing from your failures, they certainly are going to be encouraged to give it another shot.
— *Zig Ziglar*

When hard times come we easily get discouraged. But behind the clouds God is still present, and can even use them to water our souls with unexpected blessings.
— *Billy Graham*

July 1

Faith

Faith is to believe what you do not see; the reward of this faith is to see what you believe.
— *St. Augustine*

True faith goes into operation when there are no answers.
— *Elisabeth Elliot*

Faith is deliberate confidence in the character of God whose ways you may not understand at the time.
— *Oswald Chambers*

All I have seen teaches me to trust the Creator for all I have not seen.
— *Ralph Waldo Emerson*

July 2

God Will Provide
God will do the right thing at the right time. And what a difference that makes. Since you know that His provision is timely, you can enjoy the present.
— *Max Lucado*

A righteous man may have many troubles, but the Lord delivers him from them all.
— *Psalm 34:19*

It doesn't matter whether you're short of money, people, energy or time. What God invites you to do will always be greater than the resources you start with.
— *Bruce Wilkinson*

If God gave His own Son for us, how could He ever bring Himself to desert us in small things?
— *Martin Luther*

July 3

Opportunity

When God allows one door to close, He will open another door for you, revealing something bigger and better.
— *Joel Osteen*

If your ship doesn't come in, swim out to it.
— *Jonathan Winters*

Wherever there is danger, there lurks opportunity; whenever there is opportunity, there lurks danger. The two are inseparable. They go together.
— *Earl Nightingale*

I will study and get ready and someday my chance will come.
— *Abraham Lincoln*

July 4

Solving Problems

It is a common experience that a problem difficult at night is resolved in the morning after the committee of sleep has worked on it.

— *John Steinbeck*

The best time to tackle a minor problem is before it grows up.

— *Hermine Hartley*

Understand that often when you have searched in vain for a solution to a problem, you can find it by helping someone else solve his or her problem. By the time you have solved the other person's problem, you will have the insight to solve your own.

— *Napoleon Hill*

Find the essence of each situation, like a logger clearing a log jam. The pro climbs a tall tree and locates the key log, blows it and lets the stream do the rest. An amateur would start at the edge of the jam and move all the logs, eventually moving the key log. Both approaches work, but the *essence* concept saves time and effort. Almost all problems have a *key* log if we learn to find it.

— *Fred Smith*

July 5

Work

The glory of tomorrow is rooted in the drudgery of today.

— *L.B. Cowman*

You just can't be miserable as long as you are properly and enjoyably busy; there is no room for misery. Work is the best wonder drug ever devised by God.

— *Orlando Battista*

I have always found, when I was worrying, that the best thing to do was put my mind upon something, work hard and forget what was troubling me.

— *Thomas Edison*

There's no thrill in easy sailing, when the skies are clear and blue.

There's no joy in only doing things, which anyone can do.

But there is some satisfaction that is mighty sweet to take.

When you reach a destination that you thought you'd never make.

— *Spirella*

❧ July 6

Overcome Difficulties
No matter whether something is *fair* or not, you can't let it slow you down in getting to your goal and can never use it as an excuse.

— *Dawn Riley*

Tonight, when you lay your head on your pillow, forget how far you still have to go. Look instead at how far you've already come.

— *Bob Moawad*

It is a rough road that leads to the heights of greatness.

— *Seneca*

When you feel isolated, seek out someone who is alone. When you feel forsaken, comfort one who has been abandoned. When you feel impoverished, give to the poor. When you feel unloved, love a child.

— *Greg Quinn*

July 7

Best Effort

I've always made a total effort, even when the odds seemed entirely against me.
— *Arnold Palmer*

Whether our efforts are, or not, favored by life, let us be able to say, when we come near the great goal, "I have done what I could."
— *Louis Pasteur*

Winners are not always those who have finished first. A winner is someone who gives the most in preparation to reach his potential and makes every effort to perform at his highest level. There will be times when that is accomplished and you still aren't victorious; but you are a winner.
— *Dr. Gary Wiren*

The man who tried his best and failed is superior to the man who never tried.
— *Bud Wilkinson*

July 8

The Best Book
A single line in the Bible has consoled me more than all the other books I ever read.
— *Immanuel Kant*

After more than sixty years of almost daily reading of the Bible, I never fail to find it always new and marvelously in tune with the changing needs of every day.
— *Cecil B. DeMille*

Weave the unveiling fabric of God's Word through your heart and mind. It will hold strong, even if the rest of life unravels.
— *Gigi Tchividjian*

The Bible is a book in comparison with which all others in my eyes are of minor importance; and which in all my perplexities and distresses has never failed to give me light and strength.
— *General Robert E. Lee*

July 9

Overcome Fear

Once men are caught up in an event they cease to be afraid. Only the unknown frightens men.
— *Antoine de Saint-Exupery*

I made the decision long ago that to be afraid would be to diminish my life.
— *Janet Reno*

We must look fear straight in the eye and take it on. We must tell ourselves that we have too much talent, too much wisdom, too much value not to change.
— *Rick Pitino*

Fear is a thought pattern and can be changed by a process of displacement. The only thing greater than fear is faith. So I endeavor to keep my mind full of faith; faith in God and faith in myself as a child of God. I find that the more faith I have the less fear I have.
— *Norman Vincent Peale*

July 10

The Power of Positive Thinking

It's easy to have faith in yourself and have discipline when you're a winner, when you're number one. What you've got to have is faith and discipline when you're not a winner.

— *Vince Lombardi*

To keep your attitude positive, you have to feed it with positive thoughts.

— *Jack Nicklaus*

The leader must have infectious optimism, and the determination to persevere in the face of difficulties; he must also radiate confidence, even when he himself is not too certain of the outcome.

— *Field Marshall Bernard Montgomery*

You cannot achieve any goal if you have negative thoughts running through your head. You must have positive and, what might seem to others, bold thoughts.

— *Gary Player*

July 11

The Power of Commitment

As long as a person doesn't admit he is defeated, he is not defeated – he's just a little behind, and isn't through fighting.

— *Darrell Royal*

Waiting is God's school, wherein we learn some of His most valuable lessons for us.

— *Anonymous*

I have a great deal more respect for someone who keeps coming back after losing heartbreaker after heartbreaker than I do for the winner who has everything going for him.

— *Wilt Chamberlain*

There are lots of people with extraordinary natural talent who never make it. There are also lots of people with very average abilities who do. The difference is that the people in the second group have the discipline to persevere and not back down when things get difficult.

— *Mary Lou Retton*

July 12

The Adversity Advantage

By His wisdom He so orders His delays, that they prove to be far better than our hurries.
— *Charles Haddon Spurgeon*

I definitely believe that with all that I've gone through in my life with my injuries and illnesses I'm a stronger person. I'm more determined and I don't think there is anything that I can't encounter or conquer after what I've gone through.
— *Gail Devers, on battling Grave's Disease*

God allows us to have disappointments, frustrations, or even worse because He wants us to see that our joy is not in such worldly pleasures as success or money or popularity or health or sex or even in a miracle-working faith. Our joy is in the fact that we have a relationship with God.
— *Catherine Marshall*

If Joseph had never been Egypt's prisoner, he would have never been Egypt's governor. The iron chain that bound his feet brought about the golden chain around his neck.
— *L.B. Cowman*

July 13

Benefit from Failure

One of the first things I learned is that there was a relationship between screwing up and learning. The more mistakes I made, the faster I learned.
— *Michael Dell*

I am not discouraged, because every wrong attempt discarded is another step forward.
— *Thomas Edison*

At times failure is very necessary for the artist. It reminds him that failure is not the ultimate disaster. And this reminder liberates him from the mean fussing of perfectionism.
— *John Berger*

What is defeat? Nothing but education, nothing but the first step to getting better. It is defeat that turns the bones to flint and gristle to muscle and makes men invincible and forms those basic natures that are now in ascendancy in the world. Do not be afraid of defeat.
— *Vince Lombardi*

July 14

How to Pray

Prayer is not conquering God's reluctance, but taking hold of God's willingness.

— *Phillips Brooks*

Recognize that prayer brings the best results when you have sufficient faith to see yourself already in possession of the things you are praying for.

— *Napoleon Hill*

You do not have, because you do not ask God. When you ask, you do not receive, because you ask with wrong motives, that you may spend what you get on your pleasures.

— *James 4:2-3*

Let your prayer be so definite that you can say as you leave the prayer closet, "I know what I have asked from the Father, and I expect an answer."

— *Andrew Murray*

July 15

Receiving Criticism
A successful man is one who can lay a firm foundation with bricks that others throw at him.
— *David Brinkley*

Any fool can criticize, condemn and complain – and most fools do.
— *Dale Carnegie*

Always listen to experts. They'll tell you what can't be done and why. Then do it.
— *Robert Heinlein*

It is not the critic who counts. The credit belongs to the man who is actually in the arena; whose face is marred with sweat and dust and blood; who strives valiantly; who errs and comes short again and again; who knows the great enthusiasms, the great devotions and spends himself in a worthy cause and who, if he fails, at least fails while bearing greatly so that his place shall never be with those cold and timid souls who know neither victory nor defeat.
— *Theodore Roosevelt*

July 16

Worry
Worry never robs tomorrow of its sorrow, it only saps today of its joy.
— *Leo Buscaglia*

Worry makes for a hard pillow. When something's troubling you, before going to sleep, jot down three things you can do the next day to help solve the problem.
— *H. Jackson Brown, Jr.*

If you worry about what might be, and wonder what might have been, you will ignore what is.
— *Anonymous*

When I look back on these worries I remember the story of the old man who said on his deathbed that he had had a lot of trouble in life, most of which had never happened.
— *Sir Winston Churchill*

July 17

Build Your Faith

Two signposts of faith: Slow Down and Wait Here.
— *Charles Stanley*

To be possessed with an ever increasing faith one must make constant use of the faith that they have.
— *Charles Price*

How do we learn consistent faith? We learn it one day at a time. We learn it through endurance.
— *Charles Swindoll*

Strong faith is content without signs, without tokens, without marvels; it believes God's bare word and asks for no confirming miracle.
— *Charles Haddon Spurgeon*

July 18

When Bad Things Happen

The iron crown of suffering precedes the golden crown of glory.

— *Anonymous*

Although the world is full of suffering, it is also full of the overcoming of it.

— *Helen Keller*

Either He will shield you from suffering or He will give you unfailing strength to bear it. Be at peace, then, and put aside all anxious thoughts.

— *St. Francis de Sales*

Suffering and success go together. If you are succeeding without suffering, it is because others before you have suffered; if you are suffering without succeeding, it is that others after you may succeed.

— *Edward Judson*

July 19

Cheerfulness

A cheerful disposition is a fund of ready capital, a magnet for the good things of life.
— *Orison Marden*

Assume a cheerfulness you do not feel and shortly you will feel the cheerfulness you assumed.
— *Chinese proverb*

The very best medicine that a family can keep in the house is cheerfulness.
— *Anonymous*

Wondrous is the strength of cheerfulness, and its power of endurance. The cheerful man will do more in the same time, will do it better, will persevere in it longer, than the sad or sullen.
— *Thomas Carlyle*

July 20

Enemy Territory

The wise learn many things from their enemies.
— *Aristophanes*

I love my enemies for two reasons: They inspire me to recognize my weakness. They also inspire me to perfect my imperfect nature.
— *Sri Chinmoy*

Whenever you are confronted with an opponent, conquer him with love.
— *Mahatma Gandhi*

Stay open-minded, treat your attackers fairly, listen to what they say and give them your attention whenever it is appropriate. You may learn something. Furthermore, if you do not treat them as your enemies, you make it easier for them to someday become your allies and friends.
— *Kent Keith*

July 21

Eternal Life

In God's eyes, the greatest heroes of faith are not those who achieve prosperity, success and power in this life, but those who treat this life as a temporary assignment and serve faithfully, expecting their promised reward in eternity.
— *Rick Warren*

Live near to God, and all things will appear little to you in comparison with eternal realities.
— *Robert McCheyne*

Hold everything earthly with a loose hand; but grasp eternal things with a death-like grip.
— *Charles Haddon Spurgeon*

In order to keep us from becoming too attached to earth, God allows us to feel a significant amount of discontent and dissatisfaction in life – longings that will never be fulfilled on this side of eternity. We're not completely happy here because we're not supposed to be. Earth is not our final home; we were created for something much better.
— *Rick Warren*

July 22

Have Fun

We should consider every day lost in which we have not danced at least once.

— *Friedrich Nietzsche*

Do something just for fun. Pleasure is one of life's essential nutrients.

— *Cheryl Richardson*

Our minds need relaxation, and give way
  Unless we mix with work a little play.

— *Jean Moliére*

Laughing, singing and dancing are the fastest ways to transform worries into celebration. Having fun together will strengthen your family and foster easy, honest relationships among all of you. And as your children grow they are much more likely to enjoy being with the family if everyone is having a good time.

— *Judy Ford*

July 23

The Power of Confidence

To be a champion, you have to believe in yourself when nobody else will.
— *Sugar Ray Robinson*

When you have confidence, you can have a lot of fun; and when you have fun, you can do amazing things.
— *Joe Namath*

Confidence is the sexiest thing a woman can have.
— *Aimee Mullins*

No one could ever win if you had to win before you could win. So you have to win in your mind. That's what we're talking about when we're talking about confidence.
— *Dr. Bob Rotella*

July 24

Growing Through Adversity
In every adversity there is a seed to an equal or greater benefit.
— *Brig Hart*

I love the man that can smile in trouble, that can gather strength from distress and grow brave by reflection.
— *Thomas Paine*

Adversity is the state in which a man most easily becomes acquainted with himself, being free from flatterers.
— *Samuel Johnson*

If we think of ourselves as a raw diamond, we may curse the work of the cutter, grinder and polisher and may even call them *evil*. But without their efforts, our radiant beauty would never be revealed.
— *Hans Wilhelm*

July 25

Overcome Failure

Success tends to go not to the person who is error-free, because he also tends to be risk-averse. Rather it goes to the person who recognizes that life is pretty much a percentage business. It isn't making mistakes that's critical; it's correcting them and getting on with the principal task.

— *Donald Rumsfeld*

Fall seven times, stand up eight.

— *Japanese proverb*

I suffer after losses, but fortunately, I recover quickly. I have a source of power I wouldn't have without my relationship with Christ.

— *Tom Landry*

If I had to pick a time that I was most proud of him, it probably wouldn't be after a win. I've been the proudest when he came back after his disappointments, after he lost the Open in 1989 and the 1984 Masters. After the Masters, he turned around and finished second the next week at Hilton Head. To me, that tells you more about him than a win. It's how you handle the disappointments.

— *Christy Kite, Tom's wife*

Rebound Strong

July 26

The Power of Patience
On the whole, it is patience which makes the final difference between those who succeed or fail.
— *John Ruskin*

Patience is a necessary ingredient of genius.
— *Benjamin Disraeli*

At least as important as the thing we are waiting for is the work God does in us while we wait.
— *Charles Swindoll*

Patience is a key word. It is not only a willingness to work, it is the patience to work for goals long deferred. It is a willingness to work when one sees few, if any, results. A willingness to work now, for results that may not be evident until years from now.
— *Charles Kemp*

July 27

The Power of Laughter

To enhance my performance, I laugh a lot. I think laughter is the best remedy for everything.
— *Tracia Byrnes*

A person without a sense of humor is like a wagon without springs, jolted by every pebble in the road.
— *Henry Ward Beecher*

Trouble knocked at the door, but hearing a laugh within, hurried away.
— *Benjamin Franklin*

Laughter has always brought me out of unhappy situations. Even in your darkest moment, you usually can find something to laugh about if you try hard enough.
— *Red Skelton*

July 28

Overcome Weaknesses

I was the kind nobody thought could make it. I had a funny Boston accent. I couldn't pronounce my R's. I wasn't a beauty.

— *Barbara Walters*

Identify your personal limits, and then push past them. Then set new barriers, and repeat the process, again and again and again.

— *Nicole Haislett*

Change what's wrong for the better, and of course it'll feel strange at first. That's normal. Don't panic. You'll probably get worse before you get better.

— *Gary McCord*

The weaker we feel, the harder we lean on God. And the harder we lean, the stronger we grow.

— *Joni Eareckson Tada*

July 29

God Gives Us Power

Without the assistance of the Divine Being, I cannot succeed. With that assistance, I cannot fail.
— *Abraham Lincoln*

For God did not give us a spirit of timidity, but a spirit of power, of love and of self-discipline.
— *2 Timothy 1:7*

If we try to do God's will in our own strength, then we can take the credit for whatever gets accomplished. But that isn't God's way. When we let His strength work through us, then He alone will get the glory.

— *Billy Graham*

Be strong and courageous, and do the work. Do not be afraid or discouraged, for the LORD God, my God, is with you. He will not fail you or forsake you.
— *1 Chronicles 28:20*

July 30

Overcome Difficulties

Ultimately, success is not measured by first place prizes. It's measured by the road we have traveled, how you dealt with the challenges and the stumbling blocks you encountered along the way.
— *Nicole Haislett*

If you don't have the best of everything, make the best of everything you have.
— *Erk Russell*

If you don't like something change it. If you can't change it, change your attitude. Don't complain.
— *Maya Angelou*

I am willing to put myself through anything; temporary pain or discomfort means nothing to me as long as I can see that the experience will take me to a new level. I am interested in the unknown, and the only path to the unknown is through breaking barriers, an often painful process.
— *Diana Nyad*

July 31

Giving

Charity is the bone shared with the dog when you are just as hungry as the dog.
— *Jack London*

Pay goodness for evil. We should be like trees that give fruits to those who throw stones at them.
— *Leo Tolstoy*

It's easy to find unhappy people who have received much; it's hard to find unhappy people who have given much.
— *David Young*

Dad taught us in so many ways that we couldn't just be concerned about our own circumstances. We also had to be concerned about the circumstances of others. I saw my father always giving and always sharing. In hindsight, this was remarkable in that we didn't have that much to share or to give.
— *John Lewis*

August 1

The Power of Courage
No noble thing can be done without risks.
— *Michel de Montaigne*

If we insist upon being as sure as is conceivable, in every step of our course, we must be content to creep along the ground, and can never soar.
— *Cardinal John Newman*

Those who achieve greatness for God run toward the discomfort zone because that's the primary place where borders expand.
— *Bruce Wilkinson*

To become a winner and stay on top, you have to take risks and test yourself. Any time you try to reach beyond yourself, you will lose a certain amount of the time. But that is how you become the better player – a winner.
— *Fran Tarkenton*

August 2

The Best Way to Learn
I am always doing that which I cannot do, in order that I may learn how to do it.
— *Pablo Picasso*

What we learn to do, we learn by doing.
— *Aristotle*

People learn the most when teaching others.
— *Peter Drucker*

I try to learn from everyone. I look at their strengths and ask myself, "What can I do better?"
— *Annika Sorenstam*

August 3

Faith
When I cannot feel the faith of assurance, I live by the fact of God's faithfulness.
— *Matthew Henry*

Faith counts the thing done before God has acted.
— *Kenneth Hagin*

When faith is supported by facts or by logic it ceases to be faith.
— *Edith Hamilton*

Things in our lives may seem to be going all wrong, but God knows our circumstances better than we do. And He will work at the perfect moment, if we will completely trust Him to work in His own way and in His own time. Often there is nothing as godly as inactivity on our part, or nothing as harmful as restless working.
— *A.B. Simpson*

August 4

Character Required for Success

Character may be manifested in the great moments, but it is made in the small ones.
— *Phillips Brooks*

Not being beautiful was the true blessing. It forced me to develop my inner resources. The pretty girl has a handicap to overcome.
— *Golda Meir*

Having character means that you always try to do what you say you're going to do, no matter how hard it may be.
— *Pat Williams*

Nice guys may appear to finish last, but usually they're running in a different race.
— *Kenneth Blanchard and Norman Vincent Peale*

August 5

The Adversity Advantage
With every obstacle or challenge I've faced, I've managed to work through it and come out stronger and wiser.
— *Earl Woods*

Our strength often increases in proportion to the obstacles imposed upon it.
— *Paul de Rapin*

The greater the obstacle, the more glory in overcoming it.
— *Jean Moliére*

The difficulties, hardships and trials of life, the obstacles one encounters on the road to fortune are positive blessings. They knit the muscles more firmly, and teach self-reliance. Peril is the element in which power is developed.
— *William Matthews*

August 6

Resolve Conflict
Use soft words in hard arguments.
— *Henry Bohn*

Staying calm is the best way to take the wind out of an angry person's sails.
— *Anonymous*

In disagreements with loved ones, deal with the current situation. Don't bring up the past.
— *H. Jackson Brown, Jr.*

Never be disagreeable just because you disagree.
— *John Wooden*

August 7

Failure

Success is the ability to close the door on your past, regardless of your failures, and move forward.
— *Bill White*

Don't be afraid to fail. Don't waste energy to cover up failure. Learn from your failures and go on to the next challenge. It's okay to fail. If you're not failing you're not growing.
— *H. Stanley Judd*

Inside a ring or out, ain't nothing wrong with going down. It's staying down that's wrong.
— *Muhammad Ali*

It's okay to fail. Failure does not shape your personality. It's how you react to failure. Do you dust yourself off and mope? Or do you dust yourself off and become stronger the next time? And eventually you will win. It may not happen the next time. It may take a little while, but you will win in the end.
— *Tiger Woods*

August 8

The Power of Commitment

The reward goes to him who plods along unruffled, refusing to become angry with himself or the results of his efforts.

— *Bobby Jones*

They say the breaks even up in the long run, and the trick is to be a long distance runner.

— *Chuck Knox*

It's the people who stop to consider their hurt and heartache who usually fall short of their goals. Some even drop out altogether just because they experience a little disappointment or sorrow. You've got to play through your pain if you want to make it where you're going.

— *George Foreman*

The rewards for those who persevere far exceed the pain that precedes the victory.

— *Karen Livingston*

August 9

God's Will

If you're waiting on God to fill in all the shading in your picture, you will never take the first step in obeying His will. You must be prepared to trust His plan, knowing it will be full of surprises.
— *Charles Swindoll*

To be grasped, God's will must be met with a readiness to obey.
— *Suzanne de Dietrich*

Whether you turn to the right or to the left, your ears will hear a voice behind you, saying, "This is the way; walk in it."
— *Isaiah 30:21*

If you do not have clear instructions from God in a matter, pray and wait. Learn patience. Depend on God's timing. His timing is always right and best. He may be withholding directions to cause you to seek Him more intently. Don't try to skip over the relationship to get on with doing. God is more interested in a love relationship with you than He is in what you can do for Him.
— *Henry Blackaby*

August 10

Build Confidence
Plant the seeds of expectation in your mind; cultivate thoughts that anticipate achievement. Believe in yourself as being capable of overcoming all obstacles and weaknesses.
— *Norman Vincent Peale*

Lack of confidence is not the result of difficulty; the difficulty comes from a lack of confidence.
— *Seneca*

The biggest waste of mental energy is spent on self-criticism. To accomplish more, redirect your mental energy by continuously reminding yourself of all the things you do right. Belief in yourself will increase your confidence and credibility.
— *Brian Koslow*

Never mind what the *people* think of you. They may overestimate or underestimate you. Until they discover your real worth, your success depends mainly upon what you think of yourself and whether you believe in yourself. You can succeed if nobody else believes it; but you will never succeed if you don't believe in yourself.
— *William Boetcker*

August 11

Adversity

Trouble is only opportunity in work clothes.
— *Henry Kaiser*

When I was young, my mother taught me never to feel sorry for myself, because handicaps are really things to be used.
— *Stevie Wonder*

In crises the most daring course is often safest.
— *Henry Kissinger*

Your children learn how life works when you share your life with them. So let your kids learn from both your successes and your failures. Give them a taste of the struggles you face outside your home. When your children see that you're not perfect, then they can more easily share their problems and insecurities.
— *Paul Lewis*

… **August 12**

The Power of Prayer
Trouble and perplexity drive me to prayer, and prayer drives away trouble and perplexity.
— *Philip Melanchthon*

No one accomplishes so much in so little time as when he or she is praying.
— *A.E. McAdams*

Therefore I tell you, whatever you ask for in prayer, believe that you have received it, and it will be yours.
— *Mark 11:24*

When I pray, my love as a mother meets Your love as the Father. I call, and, as You answer, the problems become promises, the insecurities become wisdom, the fears become faith. You always keep Your word: You faithfully meet each need.
— *Judith Gooding*

August 13

Getting Advice

Every man, however intelligent, needs the advice of some wise friend in the affairs of life.
— *Plautus*

Write down the advice of him who loves you, though you don't like it now.
— *Ben Johnson*

Do not open your heart to every man, but discuss your affairs with one who is wise and who fears God.
— *Thomas à Kempis*

An outsider's point of view can be especially useful when you're tangled up in a problem that's obscured by a lack of clear facts. A fresh set of eyes distanced from the day-to-day reality can often provide an objective perspective.
— *Michael Dell*

❧ August 14

The Importance of Rest
For every time in stress, you need a recovering time in relaxation.
— *Emmett Miller*

There's nothing like exhaustion to make us feel really exhausted. But there's nothing like a rest to help us recharge. So if you're feeling particularly overloaded, try to find a way to take a break. A short vacation, an afternoon off, even a midday nap can work wonders.
— *Richard Leider and David Shapiro*

Tired people make bad decisions.
— *Richard Jenrette*

The places of rest that we carve out for ourselves are often where we best assess our life, our dreams, our heartaches, our faith. The power of rest is that it allows us to enjoy the journey of life, not just the destination.

— *T.D. Jakes*

August 15

The Power of Hope

I am a little deaf, a little blind, a little impotent, and on top of this are two or three abominable infirmities, but nothing destroys my hope.

— *Voltaire*

There is no medicine like hope, no incentive so great, and no tonic so powerful as expectation of something better tomorrow.

— *G.K. Chesterton*

The most profane word we use is hopeless. When you say a situation or person is hopeless, you are slamming the door in the face of God.

— *Kathy Troccoli*

Hope sees the invisible, feels the intangible and achieves the impossible.

— *Anonymous*

August 16

God Will Provide

God's work done in God's way will never lack God's supplies.

— *J. Hudson Taylor*

We are never defeated unless we give up on God.

— *Ronald Reagan*

Each of us may be sure that, if God sends us over rocky paths, He will provide us with sturdy shoes. He will never send us on any journey without equipping us well.

— *Alexander Maclaren*

We never have any surplus, but we have never lacked what we need. Sometimes it happens in strange ways, almost miraculously. We wake up without resources, with the anguish of not being able to tend to our needy. A few hours later, we almost always see the most unexpected provisions arrive from anonymous donors.

— *Mother Teresa*

August 17

When Bad Things Happen

So much has been given me, I have no time to ponder over that which has been denied.
— *Helen Keller*

I murmured because I had no shoes, until I met a man who had no feet.
— *Persian proverb*

Sometimes God calms the storm, and sometimes He lets the storm rage and calms His child.
— *Donna Wallis*

Cast all your cares on God; that anchor holds.
— *Lord Alfred Tennyson*

August 18

The Power of Kindness

Sometimes one little spark of kindness is all it takes to reignite the light of hope in a heart that's blinded by pain.

— *Barbara Johnson*

Pay bad people with your goodness; fight their hatred with your kindness. Even if you do not achieve victory over other people, you will conquer yourself.

— *Henri Frederick Amiel*

Kindness defeats everything and can never be defeated.

— *Leo Tolstoy*

A kind word, sincerely stated, can work magic, most notably in relationships where the magic is gone. We are never so sophisticated or so comfortable in a relationship that the little niceties can be neglected. If they are good enough for total strangers, they are certainly good enough for the people we love.

— *Leo Buscaglia*

August 19

Benefit from Failure

Remind yourself, in the darkest moments, that every failure is only a step toward success.
— *Og Mandino*

Often the doorway of success is entered through the hallway of failure.
— *Erwin Lutzer*

If you want to triple your success ratio, you have to triple your failure rate.
— *Harvey Mackay*

Besides the practical knowledge which defeat offers, there are important personality profits to be taken. Defeat strips away false values and makes you realize what you really want. It stops you from chasing butterflies and puts you to work digging gold.
— *William Marston*

August 20

The Power of Faith

Contrary to reason, faith regards the invisible things as already materialized.
— *Martin Luther*

If you have faith in your future, you will have power in your present.
— *John Maxwell*

Faith is the radar that sees through the fog.
— *Corrie ten Boom*

You do build in darkness if you have faith. When the light returns you have made of yourself a fortress which is impregnable to certain kinds of trouble; you may even find yourself needed and sought by others as a beacon in their dark.
— *Olga Rosmanith*

August 21

The Power of Commitment

Emotional maturity is the ability to stick to a job and to struggle through until it is finished, to endure unpleasantness, discomfort and frustration.
— *Edward Strecker*

It's not whether you get knocked down; it's whether you get up again.
— *Vince Lombardi*

So long as there is breath in me, I will persist. For now I know one of the greatest principles of success: if I persist long enough I will win.
— *Og Mandino*

We all make mistakes, but the winner knows that success comes from perseverance: trying, failing, learning and doing it again until he succeeds. Most important, a winner does not waste energy by scolding or berating himself. He keeps practicing, takes a break and tries again.
— *Judy Ford*

❦ August 22

Love
Real love has staying power. It refuses to look for ways to run away. It always opts for working through.
— *Charles Swindoll*

The highest calling of a human being is unselfish love – to love without being loved back, without any self-interest.
— *Reinhold Niebuhr*

People need loving the most when they deserve it the least.
— *John Harrigan*

If you find that you are not feeling in love anymore, be more loving.
— *Dr. Frank Pittman III*

August 23

Overcome Difficulties

Anyone who proposes to do good must not expect people to roll stones out of his way, but must accept his lot calmly even if they roll a few more upon it.
— *Albert Schweitzer*

Let us sing even when we do not feel like it, for in this way we give wings to heavy feet and turn weariness into strength.
— *J.H. Jowlett*

To welcome a problem without resentment is to cut its size in half.
— *William Ward*

I had a series of childhood illnesses: scarlet fever, pneumonia and polio. I walked with braces until I was at least nine years old. My life wasn't like the average person who grew up and decided to enter the world of sports.
— *Wilma Rudolph*

August 24

Courage
I have become more courageous by doing the very things I needed to be courageous for – first, a little, and badly. Then, bit by bit, more and better.
— *Audre Lorde*

Everyone has talent. What is rare is the courage to follow the talent to the difficult place where it leads.
— *Erica Jong*

Courage is the power to let go of the familiar.
— *Raymond Lindquist*

The true meaning of courage is to be afraid, and then, with your knees knocking and your heart racing, to step out anyway – even when that step makes sense to nobody but you.

— *Oprah Winfrey*

August 25

Maturity

Maturity is being able to pass up instant gratification for the sake of long-term rewards.
— *Pat Williams*

Maturity is the capacity to endure uncertainty.
— *John Finley*

Maturity begins when you feel you are right about something without feeling the need to prove someone else wrong.
— *Sydney Harris*

Maturity is the ability to see the big picture and not lose patience when the small details of life don't go your way.
— *Pat Williams*

August 26

Start Small

Those who would build high must begin low.
— *Matthew Henry*

The secret of getting ahead is getting started. The secret of getting started is breaking your complex overwhelming tasks into small manageable tasks, and then starting on the first one.
— *Mark Twain*

The person who moves a mountain begins by carrying away small stones.
— *Chinese proverb*

I worked my way up from dish-machine operator and fountain girl to bartender and finally, food buyer. I started teaching thirty-minute meals to move groceries. The classes were a hobby, a fun distraction – and led to TV shows, cookbooks and a monthly magazine.
— *Rachel Ray*

August 27

Certainty of God's Love

God loves us not because we are lovable, but because He is love.

— *C.S. Lewis*

There is nothing you can do to make God love you more. There is nothing you can do to make God love you less. His love is unconditional, impartial, everlasting, infinite, perfect.

— *Richard Halverson*

The Lord your God is with you, he is mighty to save. He will take great delight in you, he will quiet you with his love, he will rejoice over you with singing.

— *Zephaniah 3:17*

God does not judge us by our success. He loves each person the same. Your value and mine does not come from what we do, the clothes we wear, the house we live in or the type of car we drive. Our value comes from the fact that God made us and loves us.

— *Billy Graham*

August 28

Receiving Criticism

Welcome friendly criticism instead of reacting to it negatively. Embrace any opportunity to learn how others see you, and use it to take inventory of yourself and look for things which need improvement.

— *Napoleon Hill*

You can't let negativity get in your ear. Your ear is like an embryo. Negative ideas will grow in there if you're not careful. There are always going to be critics trying to dull your dreams. But you can't let them.

— *Russell Simmons*

When I told people I was going back into boxing at forty, they laughed. Reporters would call me on the telephone, laughing. "George, we hear you are going back to boxing." They would laugh at me. I kept training.

— *George Foreman*

The greatest pleasure in life is doing what people say you cannot do.

— *Walter Bagehot*

August 29

The Adversity Advantage

God does not send us despair in order to kill us; he sends it in order to awaken us to new life.

— *Hermann Hesse*

The door to the room of success swings on the hinges of opposition.

— *Bob Jones*

There is no normal life that is free of pain. It's the very wrestling with our problems that can be the impetus for our growth.

— *Fred Rogers*

Grief drives men into the habits of serious reflection, sharpens the understanding and softens the heart.

— *John Adams*

August 30

Ability

If you are weak, limited, ordinary, you are the best material through which God can work.
— *Henry Blackaby and Claude King*

First there are those who are winners, and know they are winners. Then there are those who are losers who know they are losers. Then there are those who are not winners, but don't know it. They're the ones for me. They never quit trying. They're the soul of our game.
— *Bear Bryant*

Whenever God designs to make His servants eminently useful, He lets them know their frailty.
— *Charles Haddon Spurgeon*

How many folks estimate difficulties in the light of their own resources and then attempt little and often fail in the little they attempt. All God's giants have been weak men and women who did great things for God because they counted on His faithfulness.
— *J. Hudson Taylor*

August 31

God Gives Us Power

I don't think there is anyone who needs God's help and grace as much as I do. Sometimes I feel so helpless and weak. I think that is why God uses me. Because I cannot depend on my strength, I rely on Him 24 hours a day.

— *Mother Teresa*

The Sovereign Lord is my strength; he makes my feet like the feet of a deer, he enables me to go on the heights.

— *Habakkuk 3:19*

God uses imperfect people who are in imperfect situations to do His perfect will.

— *David Young*

"I can do all things through Christ which strengtheneth me." The man who believes this has calm, quiet confidence, but, because his confidence is based upon God's power and not his own power, there is never the slightest speck of egotism.

— *Clinton Davidson*

September 1

Overcome Failure
I have been wounded, but not slain; I shall lie here and bleed awhile. Then I shall rise and fight again. The title of champion may from time to time fall to others more than ourselves. But the heart, the spirit and the soul of champions remains in Green Bay.
— *Vince Lombardi*

Make it a rule of life never to regret and never to look back. Regret is an appalling waste of energy. You can't build on it; it's only good for wallowing in.
— *Katherine Mansfield*

The value of being able to laugh at ourselves when we make a mistake: it helps us get on with our work.
— *Kenneth Blanchard*

There are times when I felt as if I had gone my limit. Some of my setbacks were stunners. It seemed as if I couldn't get the stamina to start over again. But every time, when I had studied things over a little, I would find a way out. No matter how hopeless things look, there is always a way out, if you look for it hard enough.

— *Lee De Forest*

September 2

Worry
Worry is like sitting in a rocking chair. It will give you something to do, but it won't get you anywhere.
— *Vance Havner*

Little minds have little worries. Big minds have no room for worries.
— *Ralph Waldo Emerson*

One of the problems with worry is that it keeps you from enjoying what you have.
— *Charles Swindoll*

Do not be anxious about anything, but in everything, by prayer and petition, with thanksgiving, present your requests to God.
— *Philippians 4:6*

September 3

The Power of Patience

Patience will achieve more than force.
— *Edward Burke*

Don't be impatient for the Lord to act! Keep traveling steadily along his pathway and in due season he will honor you with every blessing, and you will see the wicked destroyed.
— *Psalm 37:34 (TLB)*

He who waits on God never waits too long.
— *Chuck Wagner*

When things aren't going right, patience is an energized belief that things will eventually go your way. As a result, you don't give up and start to cheat or lose control or begin to take uncalled-for-risks to get the results you want right now.
— *Kenneth Blanchard*

September 4

Overcome Adversity

Never let life's hardships disturb you. After all, no one can avoid problems, not even saints or sages.
— *Nichiren Daishonin*

The best place to succeed is where you are with what you have.
— *Charles Schwab*

I could have let eighteen firings prevent me from doing what I wanted. Instead, I let them spur me on.
— *Sally Jessy Raphael*

Success is to be measured not so much by the position that one has reached in life as by the obstacles which he has overcome.
— *Booker T. Washington*

September 5

Debt

People usually borrow because they want to get rich soon; the journey should be as much fun as the destination, so why take chances.
— *Warren Buffett*

Consumer debt is an equal-opportunity marriage destroyer. It does not matter if couples are rich or poor, working class or middle class. If they accrue substantial debt, it puts a strain on their marriage.
— *Jeffrey Dew*

"Out of debt, out of danger" is, like many other proverbs, full of wisdom; but the word danger does not sufficiently express all that the warning demands. For a state of debt and embarrassment is a state of positive misery, and the sufferer is as one haunted by an evil spirit, and his heart can know neither rest nor peace till it is cast out.
— *Charles Bridges*

It is necessary for me to be extremely frugal for some time, till I have paid what I owe.
— *Benjamin Franklin*

September 6

Forgiveness
He that returns a good for evil obtains the victory.
— *Thomas Fuller*

Forgiveness does not change the past, but it does enlarge the future.
— *Paul Boese*

Be gentle and ready to forgive; never hold grudges. Remember, the Lord forgave you, so you must forgive others.
— *Colossians 3:13 (TLB)*

God forgave us without any merit on our part; therefore we must forgive others, whether or not we think they merit it.
— *Lehman Strauss*

September 7

Trust God

God is too wise to be mistaken. God is too wise to be unkind. When you can't trace His hand, that's when you must learn to trust His heart.
— *Charles Haddon Spurgeon*

Trust God for great things; with your five loaves and two fishes, He will show you a way to feed thousands.
— *Horace Bushnell*

Faith is strengthened only as we ourselves exercise it.
— *Catherine Marshall*

You will keep in perfect peace him whose mind is steadfast, because he trusts in you. Trust in the LORD forever, for the LORD, the LORD, is the Rock eternal.

— *Isaiah 26:3-4*

September 8

God's Guidance
Never dig up in unbelief what you have sown in faith. Begin with the confidence that God will guide and end with the assurance that He has guided.
— *Oswald Sanders*

I will instruct you and teach you in the way you should go; I will counsel you and watch over you.
— *Psalm 32:8-9*

There's no shame in praying for guidance. It's a sign of strength.
— *John Wooden*

When there is perplexity there is always guidance – not always at the moment we ask, but in good time, which is God's time. There is no need to fret and stew.
— *Elisabeth Elliot*

September 9

The Power of Positive Thinking
All that is necessary to break the spell of inertia and frustration is this: Act as if it were impossible to fail.
— *Dorthea Brande*

Twixt the optimist and the pessimist
    The difference is quite droll:
    The optimist the doughnut sees,
    The pessimist, the hole.
— *McLandburgh Wilson*

Your body contains the most powerful drugs in the world to treat any illness. But we can only access these drugs with positive thoughts and good humor.
— *Norman Cousins*

Nurture your mind with great thoughts. To believe in the heroic makes heroes.
— *Benjamin Disraeli*

September 10

Start Where You Are
Do not let what you cannot do interfere with what you can do.
— *John Wooden*

Nothing will be attempted if all possible obstacles must first be removed.
— *Samuel Johnson*

To be upset over what you don't have is to waste what you do have.
— *Ken Keyes, Jr.*

I am only one, but I am one. I cannot do everything, but I can do something. And that which I can do, by the grace of God, I will do.
— *D.L. Moody*

September 11

Prayer

God will either give you what you ask, or something far better.

— *Robert M'Cheyne*

We must move from asking God to take care of the things that are breaking our hearts, to praying about the things that are breaking His heart.

— *Margaret Gibb*

Every evening I turn my troubles over to God – He's going to be up all night anyway.

— *Donald Morgan*

Frequently the richest answers are not the speediest. A prayer may be all the longer on its voyage because it is bringing us a heavier freight of blessing. Delayed answers are not only trials of faith, but they give us an opportunity of honoring God by our steadfast confidence in Him under apparent repulses.

— *Charles Haddon Spurgeon*

September 12

Control Your Anger
No matter how just your words may be, you ruin everything when you speak with anger.
— *St. John Chrysostom*

Anger is a thief who steals away nice moments.
— *Joan Lunden*

Consider how much more often you suffer from your anger and grief than from those very things for which you are angry and grieved.
— *Marcus Aurelius Antoninus*

If you are patient in one moment of anger, you will escape a hundred days of sorrow.
— *Chinese proverb*

September 13

Benefit from Failure

If you're not making mistakes, then you're not doing anything. I'm positive that a doer makes mistakes.
— *John Wooden*

The man who makes no mistakes lacks boldness and the spirit of adventure. He never tries anything new. He is a brake on the wheels of progress.
— *M.W. Larmour*

A life spent making mistakes is not only more honorable but more useful than a life spent doing nothing.
— *George Bernard Shaw*

Mistakes are the usual bridge between inexperience and wisdom.
— *Phyllis Theroux*

September 14

Overcome Fear
Thinking will not overcome fear, but action will.
— *W. Clement Stone*

Instead of thinking about the fear and the negative consequences, concentrate on what you will get if you push yourself through this fear.
— *Anthony Robbins*

We only fear when we forget who walks beside us.
— *Hans Wilhelm*

I have not ceased being fearful, but I have ceased to let fear control me. I have accepted fear as a part of life – specifically the fear of change, the fear of the unknown; and I have gone ahead despite the pounding in my heart that says: Turn back, turn back, you'll die if you venture too far.
— *Erica Jong*

September 15

Perfection
Better to do something imperfectly than to do nothing flawlessly.
— *Robert Schuller*

Perfection is attained by slow degrees. It requires the hand of time.
— *Voltaire*

A man would do nothing if we waited until he could do it so well that no one could find fault.
— *Cardinal John Newman*

Understand that you won't actually ever become the best of which you are capable. That's perfection. We can't obtain perfection as I understand it. But we can work, and work hard, toward obtaining it. If you do that, you will never lose, in sports or in life.
— *John Wooden*

September 16

Overcome Difficulties
Life is ten percent what happens to you and ninety percent how you respond to it.
— *Lou Holtz*

The times are bad. Very well, you are there to make them better.
— *Thomas Carlyle*

Call the roll in your memory of conspicuously successful business giants and you will be struck by the fact that almost every one of them encountered inordinate difficulties sufficient to crush all but the gamest of spirits. Edison went hungry many times before he became famous.
— *B.C. Forbes*

When the world seems huge and dark and meaningless, focus on little things – sunlight through leaves, a cat sprawled across your knees, the taste of an apple, a dew-bright spider's web. Now is the time for gentle comforts, for friendly and familiar things.
— *Pam Brown*

September 17

The Power of Commitment

The man who can drive himself further once the effort gets painful is the man who will win.

— *Roger Bannister*

The secret to persevering is building your self-esteem so you can take rejection and move on to the next opportunity.

— *Jack Canfield*

A competitor will find a way to win. Competitors take bad breaks and use them to drive themselves just that much harder. Quitters take bad breaks and use them as reasons to give up. It's all a matter of pride.

— *Nancy Lopez*

Let us not become weary in doing good, for at the proper time we will reap a harvest if we do not give up.

— *Galatians 6:9*

September 18

The Power of Laughter

Laughter dulls the sharpest pain and flattens out the greatest stress. To share it is to give a gift of health.
— *Barbara Johnson*

Laughter gives us distance. It allows us to step back from an event, deal with it and then move on.
— *Bob Newhart*

Laughter is the sun that drives winter from the human face.
— *Victor Hugo*

A sense of humor can help you overlook the unattractive, tolerate the unpleasant, cope with the unexpected and smile through the unbearable.
— *Moshe Waldoks*

September 19

Find Contentment
Everything has its wonders, even darkness and silence, and I learn whatever state I may be in, therein to be content.
— *Helen Keller*

Until you make peace with who you are, you'll never be content with what you have.
— *Doris Mortman*

There will always be those who have more of the things we want, but there will always be those who have less, too. It's up to us to decide how to live with that fact. If we are dissatisfied, constantly comparing ourselves with those who have more, and envious of what they have, our children will likely follow in our footsteps, leading lives that are tainted by jealousy and disappointment.
— *Dorothy Nolte*

I am always content with what happens; for I know that what God chooses is better than what I choose.
— *Epictetus*

September 20

God's Grace

There is no depth to which we can fall that our Lord will not stoop to find us and reclaim us.
— *Lloyd Ogilvie*

Grace is not sought nor bought nor wrought. It is a free gift of Almighty God to needy mankind.
— *Billy Graham*

It is a high insult against the majesty of God's love when you are tempted to believe that you are beyond the mercy of God.
— *Charles Haddon Spurgeon*

Grace is the free gift of God and does not depend on our merits. If it did, it could not be called grace.
— *Hroswitha of Gandersheim*

September 21

Let Go of the Past

You can't live in the past. If you try, it prevents you from doing anything constructive today to build a better tomorrow for yourself and your family.
— *Pat Williams*

Should-haves solve nothing. It's the next thing to happen that needs thinking about.
— *Alexandra Ripley*

Finish every day and be done with it. You have done what you could. Some blunders and absurdities no doubt crept in; forget them as fast as you can. Tomorrow is a new day; begin it well and serenely and with too high a spirit to be cumbered with your old nonsense. This day is all that is good and fair. It is too dear with hopes and invitations to waste a moment on the yesterdays.
— *Ralph Waldo Emerson*

You can't change what happened yesterday no matter how hard you try, so don't spend time worrying about it.
— *Pat Williams*

September 22

The Power of Confidence

You always have to believe in yourself before others can believe in you.

— *Tommy Lasorda*

When your confidence remains unshakable, even in the face of people telling you that you're bound to fail, you'll eventually find a way to succeed.

— *Mary Lou Retton*

Jimmy taught me a long time ago that you do the best you can and don't worry about the criticisms. Once you accept the fact that you're not perfect, then you develop some confidence.

— *Rosalynn Carter*

Confidence is not thinking, "I just know that somehow things will turn out all right." It's thinking, "I know that if I do all the things necessary to succeed, I will succeed."

— *Dr. Bob Rotella*

September 23

The Adversity Advantage
My kids never had the advantage I had. I was born poor.
— *Kirk Douglas*

Better a meal of vegetables where there is love than a fattened calf with hatred.
— *Proverbs 15:17*

I thank fate for having made me born poor. Poverty taught me the true value of the gifts useful to life.
— *Anatole France*

In many ways, I think I was fortunate to grow up in poor, rather hard, circumstances, because it taught me early how to overcome adversity.
— *Gary Player*

September 24

Help Others

Do not run after happiness, but seek to do good, and you will find that happiness will run after you.
— *James Clarke*

Happiness comes not so much from doing well, but from doing well by others. If you seek and find the ways in which your work enhances the lives of others, you're going to enjoy it more.
— *Dr. Bob Rotella*

Very few burdens are heavy if everyone lifts.
— *Sy Wise*

Blessed is he who has regard for the weak; the Lord delivers him in times of trouble. The Lord will protect him and preserve his life; he will bless him in the land and not surrender him to the desire of his foes. The Lord will sustain him on his sickbed and restore him from his bed of illness.
— *Psalm 41:1-3*

September 25

Faith

Faith means trusting in advance what will only make sense in reverse.

— *Philip Yancey*

Pseudo faith always arranges a way out in case God fails it.

— *A.W. Tozer*

We have heard of many people who trusted God too little, but have you ever heard of anyone who trusted Him too much.

— *J. Hudson Taylor*

Count on the proven fact that your Father's nature is to be faithful and generous, always seeking your best.

— *Bruce Wilkinson*

September 26

When You Lose
You don't fail when you fall down, you fail when you don't get back up.
— *Earl Woods*

We all choke. You're not human if you haven't.
— *Curtis Strange*

Be brave if you lose and meek if you win.
— *Harvey Penick*

I am a winner. I just didn't win today.
— *Greg Norman*

September 27

The Power of Change
To improve is to change; to be perfect is to change often.
— *Sir Winston Churchill*

The world hates change, yet it is the only thing that has brought progress.
— *Charles Kettering*

We must always change, renew, rejuvenate ourselves; otherwise we harden.
— *Johann von Goethe*

You have to look at change as something that's exciting, something that's valuable. People with high self-esteem and passion will look at change as being stimulating and exciting, enabling them to conquer new horizons, instead of something that's going to inhibit them and make them nervous, apprehensive about both their job and their confidence in themselves.
— *Rick Pitino*

September 28

When Bad Things Happen
When any calamity has been suffered the first thing to be remembered is how much has been escaped.
— *Samuel Johnson*

These are the hard times in which a genius would wish to live. Great necessity calls forth great leaders.
— *Abigail Adams*

My early life was full of adversity, but thanks to my father's example, I turned it to positive advantage. It gave me the drive to succeed.
— *Gary Player*

Trials, suffering or tragedy may often seem the end. Yet one day, after we have walked farther down life's road, we will be able to look back and say, "Oh, Father. I see. Now I see!"
— *Jack Hayford*

September 29

Be Grateful

If you want to feel rich, just count all the things you have that money can't buy.
— *Daniel Webster*

Count your blessings every day. Make the list as long as you can. If you are fortunate enough to have it, start with health. Add the love of children and family. From there, it's easy to build the list.
— *Jeffrey Gitomer*

All you have to do is go to a hospital and hear all the simple blessings that people never before realized were blessings – being able to urinate, to sleep on your side, to be able to swallow, to scratch an itch, etc. Could exercises in deprivation educate us faster about all our blessings?
— *Abraham Maslow*

About ninety percent of the things in our lives are right and about ten percent are wrong. If we want to be happy, all we have to do is to concentrate on the ninety percent that are right and ignore the ten percent that are wrong.
— *Dale Carnegie*

September 30

God Will Provide
The LORD is close to the brokenhearted and saves those who are crushed in spirit.

— Psalm 34:18

The God of all grace, who called you to his eternal glory in Christ, after you have suffered a little while, will himself restore you and make you strong, firm and steadfast.

— 1 Peter 5:10

Then Jesus asked them, "When I sent you without purse, bag or sandals, did you lack anything?" "Nothing," they answered.

— Luke 22:35

Come to me, all you who are weary and burdened, and I will give you rest. Take my yoke upon you and learn from me, for I am gentle and humble in heart, and you will find rest for your souls.

— Matthew 11:28-29

October 1

The Power of Commitment

Perseverance is the hard work you do after you get tired of doing the hard work you already did.
— *Newt Gingrich*

Perseverance is how most things get done and deals get made, because eventually, most of the world will just give up.
— *Robert Kraft*

You need to persevere so that when you have done the will of God, you will receive what he has promised.
— *Hebrews 10:36*

Every great work, every big accomplishment, has been brought into manifestation through holding to the vision, and often just before the big achievement, comes apparent failure and discouragement.
— *Florence Shinn*

October 2

Overcome Weaknesses

When God contemplates some great work, He begins it by the hand of some poor, weak, human creature, to whom He afterwards gives aid.

— *Martin Luther*

God loves us the way we are, but He loves us too much to leave us that way.

— *Leighton Ford*

The accomplishments of those born blind are a sure proof of how much the spirit can achieve when difficulties are placed in its way.

— *George Lightenberg*

Moses spent forty years thinking he was somebody; then he spent forty years on the back side of the desert realizing he was nobody; finally, he spent the last forty years learning what God can do with a nobody.

— *D.L. Moody*

October 3

God Gives Us Power
I should be the most presumptuous blockhead upon this footstool if I for one day thought that I could discharge the duties which have come upon me, since I came to this place, without the aid and enlightenment of One who is stronger and wiser than all others.
— *Abraham Lincoln*

For God is at work within you, helping you want to obey him, and then helping you do what he wants.
— *Philippians 2:13 (TLB)*

We are never without help. We have no right to say of any good work, it is too hard for me to do, or of any sorrow, it is too hard for me to bear, or of any sinful habit, it is too hard for me to overcome.
— *Elizabeth Charles*

Reach up as far as you can, and God will reach down all the way.
— *John Vincent*

October 4

Time for Yourself
I have long been in the habit of building joy-breaks into the course of my days – allowing myself certain small pleasures for the express purpose of keeping my attitude bright.
— *Thomas Kinkade*

If you find that you are overwhelmed with responsibility to the point of mild insanity, learn to give yourself a *time-out*.
— *Joan Lunden*

For ongoing optimal energy, invest in something you love every day. Even a few minutes of pure bliss can keep you uplifted. Let's face it, you'll never find the time to do as you wish; you have to make the time – maybe in little chunks.
— *Dr. Suzanne Zoglio*

A warm bath, massage or a little pampering can go a long way toward making the week's tensions melt away. Listening to good music, eating sumptuous meals and relaxing with friends can also help restore balance amid the frenzy. These feel-good experiences can help sustain us in the long run.
— *Dr. Paul Donahue*

October 5

Adversity

The quickest way I know to lose heart is to concentrate on the things that haven't been accomplished, rather than the things that have.
— *Ron Mehl*

One day, in retrospect, the years of struggle will strike you as the most beautiful.
— *Sigmund Freud*

The longer we dwell on our misfortunes, the greater their power to harm us.
— *Voltaire*

My father was a janitor for the city of Seattle and he had a pretty hard life. Not only did he have seven children to raise, he also suffered a number of medical problems. But he took on all of these obligations that he had and he stuck to them. By watching him, I learned the value of perseverance.
— *Franklin Raines*

October 6

The Right Job

There's no such thing as a dead-end job. No matter what sort of work you do, your effort will make that job worthwhile.

— *Russell Simmons*

A dairymaid can milk cows to the glory of God.

— *Martin Luther*

There is no such thing as a perfect job. In any position you'll find some duties which, if they aren't onerous immediately, eventually will be. Success depends not merely on how well you do the things you enjoy, but how conscientiously you perform those duties you don't.

— *John Luther*

Don't assume you can't be happy unless you're doing what you love most for a living. If that were true, only a tiny portion of the world's population would be eligible for joy. The truth is that deep, abiding joy is available to anyone who learns the secret of pursuing every task with energy and dedication, as though it were a calling.

— *Thomas Kinkade*

October 7

Overcome Doubt

Never doubt in the dark what God told you in the light.
— *V. Raymond Edman*

When in doubt, just take the next small step.
— *Reginna Brett*

When we are in doubt, God will never fail to give light when we have no other plan than to please Him and to act in love for Him.
— *Brother Lawrence*

Having doubts along the way is all part of the game. We all have times when we experience frustrations. The key is to keep sticking to your plan of attack and have the patience to realize that transforming your life is a marathon, not a sprint.
— *Rick Pitino*

October 8

Benefit from Failure

Failure is the only precursor to success. Big failure, in turn, is the only precursor to big success.
— *Tom Peters*

Failure should be our teacher, not our undertaker. It is a temporary detour, not a dead end street.
— *John Maxwell*

I quit being afraid when my first venture failed and the sky didn't fall down.
— *Allen Neuharth*

Would you like me to give you a formula for success? It's quite simple, really. Double your rate of failure. You're thinking of failure as the enemy of success. But it isn't at all because you can learn from it. So go ahead and make mistakes.
— *Thomas Watson*

October 9

A Good Attitude

Attitude is a person's most important asset.
— *Tom Bradley*

People by and large become what they think about themselves.
— *Dr. Bob Rotella*

If I had a party to attend and didn't want to be there, I would play the part of someone who was having a lovely time.
— *Shirley MacLaine*

If you make a concerted effort to look at things in a more positive, upbeat manner, you will begin to see people's attitudes about you change. Because everyone likes being around positive, upbeat people. They feel lifted by them and they feed off their energy.
— *Rick Pitino*

October 10

The Adversity Advantage

God uses enlarged trials to produce enlarged saints so He can put them into enlarged places.
— *Henry and Tom Blackaby*

The ability to accept adversity and overcome it is one of the most important virtues, because it offers us the greatest opportunities for growth.
— *Gary Player*

A worldly loss often turns into spiritual gain.
— *Hazrat Khan*

Adversity carries a positive charge: it strips away all the nonessentials and forces you back to your basic strengths. Adversity shoves you down to your core values and beliefs, to the things that matter most. Back on bedrock, you find the reasons and the strength to carry on and carry through.
— *Pat Riley*

October 11

The Power of Prayer

God will give you either what you ask or something better.

— *Robert McCheyne*

This is the confidence we have in approaching God: that if we ask anything according to his will, he hears us.

— *1 John 5:14*

Prayer has given me the strength, concentration and confidence necessary to perform a seemingly impossible task.

— *Dick Chapman*

Prayer is spiritual dynamite.

— *Helen Shoemaker*

❧ October 12

Faith in God

When God calls a person to join Him in a God-sized task, faith is always required.

— *Henry Blackaby*

Real faith in God – heart faith – believes the Word of God regardless of what the physical evidence may be.
— *Kenneth Hagin*

There are so many highs and lows, peaks and valleys, whether in golf or life. My faith helps me to smooth them out.

— *Stewart Cink*

To trust God when we have securities in our iron chest is easy, but not thankworthy; but to depend on Him for what we cannot see, as it is more hard for man to do, is more acceptable to God.

— *Owen Feltham*

October 13

Receiving Criticism

Those dreamers who have been willing to press on ahead, regardless of what others were saying about them, are the ones who have changed our world.

— *Pat Williams*

Some criticism will be honest, some won't. Some praise you will deserve, some you won't. You can't let praise or criticism get to you. It's a weakness to get caught up in either one.

— *John Wooden*

To avoid criticism, do nothing, say nothing, be nothing.

— *Elbert Hubbard*

When everybody said I'd never be any good again, it just made me push on.

— *Evonne Goolagong*

October 14

Worry

At least ninety percent of the time, the things I worry about never happen. And even if they do happen, the worry has almost always done more damage to me than the thing itself.

— *Pat Williams*

To break the habit of worry, you must develop the habit of prayer.

— *Charles Stanley*

There's no sense in worrying about things you can control, because if you can control them, there's no sense worrying. And there's no sense in worrying about things you can't control, because if you can't control them, there's no sense in worrying about them.

— *Mickey Rivers*

Our Lord never worried and He was never anxious, because He was not out to realize His own ideas; He was out to realize God's.

— *Oswald Chambers*

October 15

The Power of Patience

He that can have patience can have what he will.
— *Benjamin Franklin*

The secret of patience is to do something else in the meantime.
— *Anonymous*

Patience and time do more than strength and passion.
— *Jean de la Fontaine*

Patience is not simply *teeth-clenched* endurance. It is an attitude of expectation. The farmer patiently watches his barren ground because he knows there will be results. He has patience in his labors because there will be products of his labor. So it is in the spiritual realm. God knows the final product of what is happening to us, and he would have us link patience to our faith.

— *Billy Graham*

October 16

Overcome Difficulties
It is not because things are difficult that we do not dare; it is because we do not dare that they are difficult.

— *Seneca*

Everything is difficult at first.

— *Chinese proverb*

I am not ashamed to confess that 25 years ago I was a hired laborer, hauling rails, at work on a flatboat.

— *Abraham Lincoln*

You may be looking at the mountains in your life and thinking, "If I can only conquer this one difficulty, then I won't worry about the rest." But the truth is that once you discover the excitement and passion of defeating that first mountain, you'll be anxious to get started on the next one – and so on.

— *Pat Williams*

October 17

Great Decisions

The man who insists upon seeing with perfect clearness before he decides, never decides.
— *Henri Frederick Amiel*

It is a splendid rule to refrain from making decisions when we are discouraged.
— *A.W. Tozer*

People who make great decisions have a dirty little secret. They make decisions that now and then turn out badly. They make choices that they later see were mistakes. More than you might think. There's no way around this. You can't always make a perfect call on choices that are fraught with uncertainty.
— *Charles Foster*

An incredible amount of hard feelings and conflict could be avoided if husbands would resolve not to make any decisions affecting their wives and the rest of their families without first getting their wives' consent.
— *Gary and Norma Smalley*

October 18

Vision

The great man has a vision of the future that enables him to put obstacles in perspective; the ordinary man turns pebbles in the road into boulders.

— *Henry Kissinger*

When God gives a vision, transact business on that line, no matter what it costs.

— *Oswald Chambers*

What always precedes how. You will know what God has put in your heart to do before you know how He intends to bring it about.

— *Andy Stanley*

Generally speaking, if God has given you a vision of involvement and achievement, do not expect anyone else to fully appreciate it, because it is a personal vision for you alone, and it is rare for another person to relate on that personal wave length.

— *Peter Daniels*

October 19

The Secret to Happiness

Happiness is inward, and not outward; and so, it does not depend on what we have, but on what we are.

— *Henry Van Dyke*

Happiness is produced not so much by great pieces of good fortune that seldom happen as by little advantages that occur every day.

— *Benjamin Franklin*

Just think how happy you would be if you lost everything and everyone you have right now, and then, somehow got everything back again.

— *Kobi Yamada*

Many people go through life putting off their joy and happiness. To them, goal setting means that *someday*, after they achieve something, only then will they be able to enjoy life to the fullest. The truth is that if we decide to be happy now, we'll automatically achieve more.

— *Anthony Robbins*

October 20

Illness

Like any other major experience, illness actually changes us. We think soberly, perhaps for the first time, about our past and future. Illness gives us the rarest thing in the world – a second chance, not only at health but at life itself.

— *Louis Bisch*

Diseases can be our spiritual flat tires – disruptions in our lives that seem to be disasters at the time, but end by redirecting our lives in a meaningful way.

— *Dr. Bernie Siegel*

I wouldn't wish my disease on anyone, but I feel thankful that I've gone through it. It's changed me as a person. I'm more determined. I'm a stronger person.

— *Gail Devers*

The most interesting thing about cancer is that it can be one of the most positive, life-affirming, incredible experiences ever. When somebody is in that position, he starts to really focus on his life, on his friends and family, and what's really important.

— *Lance Armstrong*

October 21

Overcome Failure

You may fail a thousand times, but success may be hiding behind the next step. You never know how close the prize is unless you continue.
— *Bob Tyler*

Maturity is the capacity to face unpleasantness, frustration, discomfort and defeat without complaint or collapse.
— *Pat Williams*

You must accept your role in a failure. Only by doing this honestly can you pinpoint why you failed and isolate what you need to work on to avoid it in the future.
— *Rick Pitino*

As a manager prior to coming to the Yankees, my win-loss record was 119 games below .500. Although I've had periods of self-doubt, and times when I did not live up to my own high expectations, I never gave in to the idea that I was somehow a failure. Had I done so, I might have completely stopped believing in myself and the possibility of realizing my dream – a World Series championship.
— *Joe Torre*

October 22

The Adversity Advantage
It is because I have lived a most difficult life that I could do this.
— *Oksana Baiul, on winning a gold medal at the 1994 Olympics*

Adversity is the breakfast of champions.
— *Rick Godwin*

The fact that there have been difficulties and hardships makes my family closer.
— *John F. Kennedy, Jr.*

He that wrestles with us strengthens our nerves and sharpens our skills. Our antagonist is our hope.
— *Edmund Burke*

October 23

Benefits of Exercise

Walking is man's best medicine.
— *Hippocrates*

Running is relaxing. I can think out problems more clearly when I'm running by myself.
— *Jim Ryun*

It is remarkable how one's wits are sharpened by physical exercise.
— *Pliny the Younger*

Physical activity can be a terrific thing to immerse yourself in; not only do you relax your mind, but you strengthen your body.
— *Napoleon Hill*

October 24

A Happy Marriage
Straighten your problems out before you go to bed. That way you will wake up smiling.
— *Louis Fromm*

Every enduring marriage involves an unconditional commitment to an imperfect person.
— *Gary Smalley and John Trent*

In lovers' quarrels, the party that loves most is always most willing to acknowledge the greater fault.
— *Sir Walter Scott*

God is supremely concerned about our happiness – yours and mine. But in His wisdom He knows that self-centered people are never happy people. So in ordaining and blessing marriage, God certainly knew He was creating the world's best climate for character development. Intimate daily living with another human forces us out of our little self-centered world.
— *Catherine Marshall*

October 25

The Power of Action

Whenever we do what we can, we immediately can do more.
— *James Clarke*

Action is the antidote to despair.
— *Joan Baez*

Don't judge each day by the harvest you reap, but by the seeds you plant.
— *Robert Louis Stevenson*

Taking action can work a peculiar magic. It can cure you (at least for the length of the performance) of a whole variety of ailments. Migraine headaches, miserable colds or toothaches will suddenly disappear as you're up there going through your paces.
— *Barbara Harris*

October 26

Friends

Our greatest wealth is not measured in terms of riches but relationships.
— *Oliver Cromwell*

The best time to make friends is before you need them.
— *Ara Parasheghian*

Your job won't take care of you when you are sick. Your friends will. Stay in touch.
— *Reginna Brett*

A true friend knows your weaknesses but shows you your strengths; feels your fears but fortifies your faith; sees you anxieties but frees your spirit; recognizes your disabilities but emphasizes your possibilities.
— *William Ward*

October 27

The Power of Commitment
Never give up your dream, because it's the process of striving for your dreams that makes life interesting and enjoyable.
— *Patrick Cohn*

Perhaps there is no more important component of character than steadfast resolution. The boy who is going to make a great man must make up his mind to win in spite of a thousand repulses or defeats.
— *Theodore Roosevelt*

Most people give up just when they're about to achieve success. They quit on the one-yard line. They give up at the last minute of the game, one foot from a winning touchdown.
— *Ross Perot*

Press on. Obstacles are seldom the same size tomorrow as they are today.
— *Robert Schuller*

October 28

Overcome Adversity

Opportunities don't present themselves in ideal circumstances. If you wait for all the lights to turn green, you will never leave your driveway.

— *John Maxwell*

Pain and suffering are inevitable in our lives, but misery is an option.

— *Chip Beck*

Man is fond of counting his troubles, but he does not count his joys. If he counted them up as he ought to, he would see that every lot has enough happiness provided for it.

— *Fyodor Dostoevsky*

People are always blaming their circumstances for what they are. I don't believe in circumstances. The people who get on in this world are the people who get up and look for the circumstances they want, and, if they can't find them, make them.

— *George Bernard Shaw*

October 29

Risks

A lot of successful people are risk-takers. Unless you're willing to do that, to have a go, to fail miserably, and have another go, success won't happen.
— *Phillip Adams*

He who risks and fails can be forgiven. He who never risks and never fails is a failure in his whole being.
— *Paul Tillich*

If you risk nothing then you risk everything.
— *Geena Davis*

Sticking your neck way out does not guarantee success. But to fail to stick your neck way out does guarantee beyond a shadow of a doubt that you will never be a Stanley Marcus or Donna Karan. The mad do often fail. Yet they are responsible for all the world's great successes.

— *Tom Peters*

October 30

Faith

Faith is the capacity to trust God while not being able to make sense out of everything.

— *James Kok*

Faith means not worrying.

— *John Dewey*

Faith does not operate in the realm of the possible. There is no glory for God in that which is humanly possible. Faith begins where man's power ends.

— *George Müller*

Hope is the ability to listen to the music of the future. Faith is the courage to dance to it in the present.

— *Peter Kuzmic*

October 31

Solving Problems

After investigating a problem in all directions, ideas come unexpectedly, without effort, like an inspiration.

— *H.L. von Helmholtz*

The more choices you have, the better your solution to a problem is likely to be. As you start your attack on a problem, therefore, you keep asking, not merely, "Is there another alternative?" You ask, "How many more alternatives are there?" The difference between the fair problem solver and the first-rate one shows up here.

— *Edward Hodnett*

When you move and when you are lightly puffing, you actually have an increased amount of oxygen inside your skull and it makes you think smarter. Often, people can find a solution to a problem while they are walking, because there is more oxygen upstairs.

— *John Tickell*

Consider each problem separately. You're less likely to become rattled.

— *Mary Mills*

November 1

Opportunities in Disguise

To find a big opportunity, seek out a big problem.
— *H. Jackson Brown, Jr.*

You can always build opportunity out of tragedy.
— *Thomas Edison, on his warehouse burning*

A pessimist sees the difficulty in every opportunity; an optimist sees the opportunity in every difficulty.
— *Sir Winston Churchill*

Among the humble and great alike, those who achieve success do so not because fate and circumstance are especially kind to them. Often the reverse is true. They succeed because they take whatever has been given to them and go on to make the most of their best.

— *Sidney Greenberg*

November 2

Benefit from Failure

There are no triumphs without setbacks. Recognize this, and you're less likely to be brought down by one failure, or a series of disappointments.

— *Joe Torre*

There is no disgrace in defeat. Champions are born in the labor of defeat.

— *Bill Tilden*

Failure is part of learning. Fear of failure can paralyze you. If you don't risk looking ridiculous or inept or even stupid sometimes, you may stay secure, but you'll also stay the same. By avoiding failure, you're also avoiding life's richness.

— *Maria Shriver*

There is no such thing as defeat, except when it comes from within. As long as a person doesn't admit he is defeated, he is not defeated – he's just a little behind and isn't through fighting.

— *Darrell Royal*

November 3

When Bad Things Happen

Many who seem to be struggling with adversity are happy; many, amid great affluence, are utterly miserable.

— *Marcus Claudius Tacitus*

Everything good that has happened to me has happened as a result of something bad.

— *Harry Caray*

If you ever start feeling sorry for yourself, visit a children's hospital. I'm active in the Elks Club, and we visit kids with cerebral palsy and other developmental disorders. I watch them trying to take a bite of food or lift a glass of water or write their names, and I think, even though I've had three heart attacks, I'm in perfect condition.

— *Robert Haas*

Some people are always grumbling because roses have thorns; I am thankful that thorns have roses.

— *Alphonse Karr*

November 4

Handicaps
I thank God for my handicaps for, through them, I have found myself, my work and my God.
— *Helen Keller*

My mother never let me use my deafness as an excuse. We had a positive environment, where if you fail, just try again.
— *Heather Whitestone*

The truth is, I'm sort of lucky to have this body because it forced me to find my strength and beauty within.
— *Aimee Mullins, amputee*

Rebellion against your handicaps gets you nowhere. Self-pity gets you nowhere. One must have the adventurous daring to accept oneself as a bundle of possibilities and undertake the most interesting game in the world – making the most of one's best.
— *Harry Emerson Fosdick*

November 5

God Gives Us Power
My flesh and my heart may fail, but God is the strength of my heart and my portion forever.
— *Psalm 73:26*

What God expects us to attempt, He also enables us to achieve.
— *Stephen Olford*

The one who is in you is greater than the one who is in the world.
— *1 John 4:4*

When we do what we can, God will do what we can't.
— *Anonymous*

November 6

Strong Character
Always choose the hard right over an easy wrong.
— *Robert Dedman*

Making a decision usually means taking one of two roads. One is doing the right thing. To take the other road, you have to sit back and spin a story around the decision or action you are taking. If you find yourself thinking up an elaborate justification for what you are doing, you are not doing the right thing.
— *Wayne Sales*

If you have not been tested by fire, you do not know who you are.
— *Laurie Beth Jones*

Dignity and honor always get tested at times when we really wish they wouldn't. This is precisely the reason why maintaining a sense of honor can be so challenging. Everything is going along as well as could be hoped for and then – whammo! – adversity strikes. But what a sweet victory it is when in such times, you handle yourself in a way you will never regret.
— *Gary Player*

November 7

Resolve Conflict

If you're in an argument, try to see the other point of view. If you don't agree, you don't agree; just don't let emotions get the best of you.
— *Yogi Berra*

Don't fight a battle if you don't gain anything by winning.
— *General George Patton*

He who establishes his argument by noise and command, shows that his reason is weak.
— *Michel de Montaigne*

No matter how hard-fought the issue, never get personal. Don't say or do anything that may come back to haunt you on another issue, another day.
— *George Bush*

November 8

The Power of Positive Thinking
People who succeed speak well of themselves to themselves.

— *Laurie Beth Jones*

If you think you can't do something, chances are you won't be able to. Conversely, the power of positive thinking can turn an adverse situation into a prime opportunity for heroism.

— *Tiger Woods*

As a quarterback I have to be an optimist and live my life almost in denial. If I ever took a realistic look at some of the situations I'm faced with as an athlete, I would have to give up. The odds can sometimes be insurmountable. But as a quarterback, rather than looking at what kind of desperate situation I'm in, I try to look at how I will come through and win the game.

— *Drew Bledsoe*

I had a vision I could succeed. You have to believe that you can succeed, believe that you can be whatever your heart desires and be willing to work for it.

— *Oprah Winfrey*

November 9

The Adversity Advantage

Out of suffering have emerged the strongest souls; the most massive characters are seared with scars.
— *Edwin Chapin*

Our real blessings often appear to us in the shape of pains, losses and disappointments; but let us have patience, and we soon shall see them in their proper figures.
— *Joseph Addison*

Use any time when you aren't on center stage to strengthen your powers of perception. Even being on the bench or working around the periphery of the Lakers was like attending a master class in professional basketball.
— *Pat Riley*

It is the wounded oyster that mends its shell with pearl.
— *Ralph Waldo Emerson*

November 10

The Power of Patience

In any contest between patience and power, bet on patience.

— *W.B. Prescott*

Great things come slowly but they last.

— *Harry Emerson Fosdick*

Where there is patience and humility there is neither anger nor worry.

— *St. Francis of Assisi*

Grass that is here today and gone tomorrow does not require much time to mature. A big oak tree that lasts for generations requires much more time to grow and mature. God is concerned about your life through eternity. Allow Him to take all the time He needs to shape you for His purposes. Larger assignments will require longer periods of preparation.

— *Henry Blackaby*

November 11

How to Pray

When we pray, it is far more important to pray with a sense of the greatness of God than with a sense of the greatness of the problem.

— *Evangeline Blood*

Pray the largest prayers. You cannot think a prayer so large that God in answering it, will not wish you had made it larger. Pray not for crutches but wings.

— *Phillips Brooks*

If you believe, you will receive whatever you ask for in prayer.

— *Matthew 21:22*

In your prayers, above everything else, beware of limiting God, not only through unbelief but also by thinking you know exactly what He can do. Learn to expect the unexpected, beyond all that you ask or think.

— *L.B. Cowman*

November 12

The Power of Laughter
You can turn painful situations around through laughter. If you can find humor in anything – even poverty – you can survive it.
— *Bill Cosby*

Life's too short to walk around with your teeth gritted all the time. I like to joke. I like to laugh.
— *Bill Parcells*

A good laugh is sunshine in a house.
— *William Thackeray*

During the hard times in my life, laughter has been the language of hope.
— *Barbara Johnson*

November 13

God's Will

Obey God one step at a time, then the next step will come into view.

— *Catherine Marshall*

I have come to the place in my life that, if the assignment I sense God is giving me is something that I know I can handle, I know it probably is *not* from God.

— *Henry Blackaby*

The struggle of not doing what God has called us to do makes us weary.

— *Steve Van Winkle*

God's way is always right. It doesn't always make sense – in fact, it is often mysterious. It can seldom be explained. It isn't always pleasurable and fun. But I have lived long enough to realize that His way is always right.

— *Charles Swindoll*

November 14

God Will Provide

I pray hard, work hard and leave the rest to God.
— *Florence Griffith Joyner*

When you have shut the doors, and darkened your room, remember never to say that you are alone; for God is within.
— *Epictetus*

In the greatest difficulties, in the heaviest trials, in the deepest poverty and necessities, God has never failed me: the financial balance for the entire Inland China Mission yesterday was twenty-five cents. Praise the Lord! Twenty-five cents – plus all the promises of God.
— *J. Hudson Taylor*

"For I know the plans I have for you," declares the Lord, "plans to prosper you and not to harm you, plans to give you hope and a future."
— *Jeremiah 29:11*

November 15

Overcome Difficulties

Those who feel discouraged by hard conditions should remember that most successful men have started under discouraging conditions.
— *Theodore Vail*

When a man is pushed, tormented, defeated, he has a chance to learn something; he has been put on his wits. He has gained facts, learned his ignorance, is cured of the insanity of conceit, has got moderation and real skill.
— *Ralph Waldo Emerson*

Adversity will usually start to resolve itself when you begin to take action.
— *Rick Pitino*

The more I see of the real champions and succeeders in this world, the more I become convinced that natural aptitude and talent are not the secrets to their success. Rather it is the ability to overcome obstacles that makes the difference between success and failure.
— *Robert Backman*

November 16

Failure

Don't hide your failures and mistakes. Bury them in full public view with due humility and contrition. Who has the heart to castigate a repentant sinner?
— *Milton Roedel*

Losing is no disgrace if you've given your best.
— *Jim Palmer*

Any man worth his salt will stick up for what he believes right, but it takes a slightly bigger man to acknowledge instantly and without reservation that he is in error.
— *General Peyton March*

When you're wrong, admit it. Many people feel it diminishes them to say, "I was wrong." The truth is we increase our stature when we are big enough to admit mistakes. Leaders who can honestly admit they were wrong are the most respected and admired leaders of all.
— *Pat Williams*

November 17

The Power of Faith

If you've got just a little bit of faith as a grain of mustard seed, and begin to praise God, that faith will mount up, until fear won't be able to stay in your heart.

— *Jack Coe*

Whenever you see real, raw, unpretentious faith in anybody, watch them. They are giant killers, mountain movers and life changers.

— *T.D. Jakes*

Now faith is being sure of what we hope for and certain of what we do not see.

— *Hebrews 11:1*

Faith is a living, bold trust in God's grace, so certain of God's favor that it would risk death a thousand times trusting in it. Such confidence and knowledge of God's grace makes you happy, joyful and bold in your relationship to God and all creatures.

— *Martin Luther*

November 18

Financial Freedom

Resolve not to be poor; whatever you have, spend less.
— *Samuel Johnson*

Fearing that we may miss a *golden opportunity,* we often buy things we can't afford – and regret it later.
— *Ron Blue*

If you're unable to pay your credit cards in full each month, cancel your cards. Cut them into pieces and throw them away. Then establish a plan to pay off any existing credit card or consumer debt balances within the year.

— *Elaine St. James*

A reasonable cash reserve (approximately three months of income) should be maintained for emergencies such as layoffs, illnesses and emergency giving.

— *Larry Burkett*

November 19

God's Guidance

We should make plans – counting on God to direct us.

— Proverbs 16:9 (TLB)

Show me your ways, O Lord, teach me your paths; guide me in your truth and teach me, for you are God my Savior, and my hope is in you all day long.

— Psalm 25:4-5

There is nothing so small but that we may honor God by asking His guidance of it, or insult Him by taking it into our own hands.

— John Ruskin

I know not the way God leads me, but well do I know my Guide.

— Martin Luther

November 20

The Power of Forgiveness
The power of reconciliation is stronger than revenge. It is amazing how forgiveness unloads the weapon in the other person's hand.
— *Charles Swindoll*

A man that studies revenge keeps his wounds green, which otherwise would heal and do well.
— *Sir Francis Bacon*

When you hold resentment toward another, you are bound to that person or condition by an emotional link that is stronger than steel. Forgiveness is the only way to dissolve that link and get free.
— *Catherine Ponder*

I've had a few arguments with people, but I never carry a grudge. You know why? While you're carrying a grudge, they're out dancing.
— *Buddy Hackett*

November 21

Adversity

Most of my major disappointments have turned out to be blessings in disguise. So whenever anything bad does happen to me, I kind of sit back and feel, well, if I give this enough time, it'll turn out that this was good, so I won't worry about it too much.
— *William Gaines*

Fire is the test of gold; adversity is the test of strong men.
— *Seneca*

God created the world out of nothing, and as long as we are nothing, He can make something out of us.
— *Martin Luther*

Being myself no stranger to suffering, I have learned to relieve the suffering of others.
— *Virgil*

November 22

Overcome Fear

To fear the unknown is to never know the wonder of newfound things.
— *Gary Player*

Many of our fears are tissue-paper-thin, and a single courageous step would carry us clear through them.
— *Brendan Francis*

Daniel looked into the face of his God, and would not fear the face of a lion.
— *Charles Haddon Spurgeon*

There's only one way I know to overcome fear, and that is to stare your fear in the face and keep moving in the direction of your dream – no matter how much your heart may be pounding, your knees shaking or your brain telling you to turn back.
— *Pat Williams*

November 23

The Power of Commitment

An athlete's greatest glory lies not in never falling, but in rising every time he falls.
— *Norm Van Brocklin*

I am not the smartest or most talented person in the world, but I succeeded because I kept going, and going, and going.
— *Sylvester Stallone*

Often, what seems impossible in the short term becomes very possible in the long term if you persist. In order to succeed, we need to discipline ourselves to consistently think long term.
— *Anthony Robbins*

Don't give up whatever you're trying to do – especially if you're convinced that you're botching it up. Giving up reinforces a sense of incompetence, going on gives you a commitment to success.
— *George Weinberg*

November 24

Confidence

It's when things get tough, as they invariably do, that people with real talent separate themselves from the competition by finding ways to think confidently despite the hard times.
— *Dr. Bob Rotella*

Winners look like winners. Exude a confident image, even if you don't feel confident.
— *Stan Smith*

Confidence means being able to laugh at yourself.
— *Bill Russell*

I've gone through life believing in the strength and competence of others; never in my own. Now, dazzled, I discovered that my capacities were real. It was like finding a fortune in the lining of an old coat.
— *Joan Mills*

November 25

Serve Others

The only really happy people are those who have learned how to serve.
— *Albert Schweitzer*

When people are serving, life is no longer meaningless.
— *John Gardner*

The best way to find yourself is to lose yourself in the service of others.
— *Mahatma Gandhi*

The best antidote I know for comparison compulsion (or status-symbol syndrome, as it's also known) is service. Not serving just anyone, but serving people who can't give you anything of value in return.
— *Kerry and Chris Shook*

November 26

Renewal

Simple, little things can rest your soul, like eating in the park and lying on the grass rather than sitting in the same dim cubbyhole at work.

— *T.D. Jakes*

Short periods of relaxation throughout the day can break tension and give your subconscious a chance to work. Read a magazine article; listen to a language tape; work on a crossword puzzle. This is not wasting time; it is keeping your mind in top condition through relaxation.

— *Napoleon Hill*

God gave us the Sabbath to protect us from overload. He designed it as a day to restore us – spiritually, mentally, emotionally and physically.

— *Steve and Mary Farrar*

One of the symptoms of an approaching nervous breakdown is the belief that one's work is terribly important, and that to take a vacation would bring all kinds of disaster. If I were a medical man, I should prescribe a vacation to any patient who considered his work important.

— *Bertrand Russell*

November 27

Start Where You Are

When we cannot do what and where we would, we must do what and where we can.
— *Matthew Henry*

Being unready and ill-equipped is what you have to expect in life. You must always do with less than you need in a situation vastly different from what you would have chosen as appropriate for your special endowments.
— *Charlton Ogburn, Jr.*

Don't wait until you *feel good* to move. It's the movement that creates the good feelings.
— *Deborah Shaw*

There are two kinds of *disabled* persons: Those who dwell on what they have lost and those who concentrate on what they have left.
— *Thomas Szasz*

November 28

Overcome Failure
Train yourself to accept the fact that as a human being you are prone to mistakes. Take pride in being emotionally resilient and mentally tough.
— *Dr. Bob Rotella*

Having harvested all the knowledge and wisdom we can from our mistakes and failures, we should put them behind us and go ahead.
— *Edith Johnson*

All good men make mistakes, but a good man yields when he knows his course is wrong, and repairs the evil.
— *Sophocles*

My own success was attended by quite a few failures along the way. But I refused to make the biggest mistake of all: worrying too much about making mistakes.
— *Kemmons Wilson*

November 29

Receiving Criticism

You can't please everybody. Don't let criticism worry you. Don't let your neighbors set your standards.
— *Robert Louis Stevenson*

When I decided to go into politics I weighed the costs. I would get criticism. But I went ahead. So when virulent criticism came I wasn't surprised. I was better able to handle it.
— *Herbert Hoover*

I stood in front of a speech class and said, "I plan to make my living with my oratory skills, and I'd like to be a talk show host." There was a pause, then the most incredible laughter you've ever heard in your life.
— *Arsenio Hall*

If I tried to answer all the criticisms of me and all the attacks leveled at me, this office would be closed to all other business. My job is not pleasing men, but doing the best I can. If the end proves me to have been right, then all that is said about me now will amount to nothing.
— *Abraham Lincoln*

November 30

Worry

When I am anxious it is because I am living in the future. When I am depressed it is because I am living in the past.

— *Jimmy R.*

I may be a strange animal but I don't worry. Whenever I make a decision, I start out recognizing there's a strong likelihood I'm going to be wrong. All I can do is the best I can. To worry puts obstacles in the way of clear thinking.

— *Fletcher Byrom*

Anxiety is often a red light on the mind's dashboard that tells us we are not expressing our needs to God and trusting Him to provide.

— *Richard Lovelace*

Worry is a destructive process of occupying the mind with thoughts contrary to God's love and care. The cure is to fill the mind with thoughts of God's power, His protection and His goodness.

— *Norman Vincent Peale*

December 1

Learning

Anything worth doing is worth doing poorly, until you can learn to do it well.
— *Steve Brown*

Every man I meet is in some way my superior, and I can learn from him.
— *Ralph Waldo Emerson*

All things are difficult before they are easy.
— *Thomas Fuller*

Learn from others. Learn from people who have made the journey before you. Learn from their wisdom.
— *Rick Pitino*

December 2

Help from Others

Be brave enough to accept the help of others.
— *Melba Colgreve, Harold Bloomfield and Peter McWilliams*

Men can do jointly what they cannot do singly; and the union of minds and hands, the concentration of their power, becomes almost omnipotent.
— *Daniel Webster*

Many receive advice; only the wise profit by it.
— *Publilius Syrus*

The secret of survival is not simply enjoying life's joys and enduring its sorrows, it is in sharing both with others. We gain perspective by having somebody at our side. We gain objectivity. We gain courage in threatening situations. Having others near tempers our dogmatism and softens our intolerance. We gain another opinion.
— *Charles Swindoll*

December 3

The Adversity Advantage
Adversity reveals genius, prosperity conceals it.
— *Horace*

If we study the lives of great men and women we find that, invariably, greatness was developed, tested and revealed through the darker periods of their lives.
— *Joan Rivers*

God will not permit any troubles to come upon us, unless He has a specific plan by which great blessing can come out of the difficulty.
— *Peter Marshall*

Consider it pure joy, my brothers, whenever you face trials of many kinds, because you know that the testing of your faith develops perseverance. Perseverance must finish its work so that you may be mature and complete, not lacking anything.
— *James 1:2-4*

December 4

Build Your Faith

He who lives up to a little faith shall have more faith.
— *Thomas Brooks*

Feed your faith and your doubts will starve to death.
— *Anonymous*

Obey one step at a time, then the next step will come into view. God will not give us a blueprint of the future; He still insists that our walk be step by step in faith.
— *Catherine Marshall*

You know that if you get in the water and have nothing to hold on to, but try to behave as you would on dry land, you will drown. But if, on the other hand, you trust yourself to the water and let go, you will float. And this is exactly the situation of faith.
— *Alan Watts*

December 5

Do the Impossible

When we're surrounded by things that look impossible, making a simple choice to do something that's possible is a powerful thing to do.

— *Melody Beattie*

Impossibilities vanish when a man and his God confront a mountain.

— *Robert Schuller*

I think of what has to be done, not of whether it can be done.

— *George Allen*

One of the greatest discoveries a man makes, one of his great surprises, is to find he can do what he was afraid he couldn't do.

— *Henry Ford*

December 6

Commitment

Victory belongs to the most persevering.
— *Napoléon Bonaparte*

If the goal is significant, it is inevitable that unforeseen mishaps and emergencies will appear along the way. When the scope and demands of a project are extensive, you can't possibly anticipate all contingencies. These challenges test your allegiance to your goal. By having a deep dedication to your mission, you will keep going when others have given up.
— *Marilyn Tam*

It took me twenty years to become an overnight success.
— *Eddie Cantor*

Determination is what keeps us hammering away. Determined people possess the stamina and courage to pursue their ambitions despite criticism, ridicule or unfavorable circumstance. In fact, discouragement usually spurs us on to greater things.
— *Harvey Mackay*

December 7

Overcome Weaknesses

Don't be frustrated by your own inexperience. All green things grow and blossom eventually with enough nurturing.

— *Anonymous*

Focus on remedies, not faults.

— *Jack Nicklaus*

Lean, thin hair, can't be photographed very well, not much personality and so forth. Also dances.
— *Anonymous, film studio executive commenting on Fred Astaire after a 1928 screen test*

To change a behavior, we must be willing to experience a certain degree of discomfort.

— *Marie Lindquist*

❦ December 8

God Gives Us Power
For the Lord your God is the one who goes with you to fight for you against your enemies to give you victory.

— Deuteronomy 20:4

Think big, talk big, act big. Because we have a big God.

— Kathryn Kuhlman

I am the vine; you are the branches. If a man remains in me and I in him, he will bear much fruit; apart from me you can do nothing.

— John 15:5

The task ahead of us is never as great as the Power behind us.

— Anonymous

December 9

Overcome Difficulties
One of the keys to success lies in understanding the nature of the obstacle before you, then using it to your advantage. Find out how that obstacle can make you stronger. Learn from it. Grow.
— *Heather Whitestone, Miss America 1994, who is deaf*

If you would not have affliction visit you twice, listen at once to what it teaches.
— *James Burgh*

I view adversity, in all its forms, as a test of my faith in God. If I develop the habit of trusting God on a regular basis with the myriad little problems that constitute daily life, then I'm prepared when the larger issue of adversity arises.
— *Bobby Bowden*

One method I use to discover the treasure in my personal trials is to write on a piece of paper a list of my past trials and what possible benefits have come from each of them.
— *Gary and Norma Smalley*

December 10

The Power of Enthusiasm
Everyone faces hardships along their chosen path. What carries them through? Makes them work and pray with no thought of quitting? Enthusiasm.
— *Conrad Hilton*

Enthusiasm is the greatest asset in the world. It beats money and power and influence. It is faith in action.
— *Henry Chester*

Those folks who succeed simply remain enthusiastic longer than those who fail.
— *Ralph Waldo Emerson*

Every man is enthusiastic at times. One man has enthusiasm for thirty minutes, another has it for thirty days – but it is the man that has it for thirty years who makes a success of his life.
— *Edward Butler*

December 11

Benefit from Failure

No man ever progressed to greatness but through great mistakes.
— *Frederick Robertson*

Failure jolts us out of our routines and forces us to look for fresh approaches.
— *Roger von Oech*

You really don't know what your true potential is until you've pushed yourself beyond your limits. You have to fail a couple of times to really find out how far you can go.
— *Debi Thomas*

We seem to gain wisdom more readily through our failures than through our successes. We always think of failure as the antithesis of success, but it isn't. Success often lies just the other side of failure.
— *Leo Buscaglia*

December 12

Prayer

The best disposition for praying is that of being desolate, forsaken, stripped of everything.
> — *St. Augustine*

Prayer is asking for rain; faith is carrying the umbrella.
> — *Sir John Mason*

Any concern too small to be turned into a prayer is too small to be made into a burden.
> — *Corrie ten Boom*

Prayer should be the key of the day and the lock of the night.
> — *Thomas Fuller*

December 13

Great Potential

A human being doesn't know how far he can go until he's pushed himself to the limit.
— *Bob Mattick*

Most people have no idea how far below their potential they're living. God has created us with almost limitless possibilities. If you look at your life and you aren't just a little surprised by how far you've come, then you probably aren't growing at the rate you should, and it's time to try the impossible.
— *John Maxwell*

When someone is pursuing their dream, they'll go far beyond what seems to be their limitation. The potential that exists within us is limitless and largely untapped. When you think of limits, you create them.
— *Robert J. Kriegel and Louis Patler*

Riches are what you have, but wealth is what you are. You are wealthy in opportunities, wealthy in creativity and wealthy in the chance to prioritize your life, maximize your potential, and reassess your strengths. You are wealthy because God loves you.
— *T.D. Jakes*

December 14

Courage
Courage grows by daring, fear by holding back.
— *Publilius Syrus*

Courage is doing what you're afraid to do. There can be no courage unless you're scared.
— *Eddie Rickenbacker*

He who loses wealth loses much; he who loses a friend loses more; but he who loses his courage loses all.
— *Miguel de Cervantes*

Success is never final. Failure is never fatal. It's courage that counts.
— *John Wooden*

December 15

When Bad Things Happen

You can overcome anything. It takes having an obstacle to learn and grow.
— *Orlando Bloom*

It has been my philosophy of life that difficulties vanish when faced boldly.
— *Isaac Asimov*

Greatness comes not when things always go good for you, but when you are really tested, when you take some knocks, some disappointments, when sadness comes. Because only if you have been in the deepest valleys can you ever know how magnificent it is to be on the highest mountain.
— *Richard Nixon*

The truth is that our finest moments are most likely to occur when we are feeling deeply uncomfortable, unhappy, or unfulfilled. For it is only in such moments, propelled by our discomfort, that we are likely to step out of our ruts and start searching for different ways or truer answers.
— *M. Scott Peck*

❧ December 16

Pressure

The real key to relieving stress is gaining control over irritants you have the power to change and accepting those you don't.

— *Dr. Paul Rosch*

Sometimes, all we need to do to de-stress is change the tape that runs in our heads. Most of us have a habit of making problems worse by saying things to ourselves like, "This is terrible," or, "I have really screwed up." Instead, say supportive and positive things to yourself, such as, "I can deal with this."

— *Frederic Luskin*

Stress is an ignorant state. It believes that everything is an emergency.

— *Natalie Goldberg*

It's important that you don't fear pressure: You should embrace it. It brings out the best in all of us. You want it every day of your working life. You want to feel that each day you are under a microscope, that you are involved in something that's important.

— *Rick Pitino*

December 17

Purpose
A difficult crisis can be more readily endured if we retain the conviction that our existence holds a purpose – a cause to pursue, a person to love, a goal to achieve.
— *John Maxwell*

You weren't an accident. You weren't mass produced. You aren't an assembly-line product. You were deliberately planned, specifically gifted and lovingly positioned on the Earth by the Master Craftsman.
— *Max Lucado*

The secret of success is constancy of purpose.
— *Benjamin Disraeli*

If you feel inordinately weighted down by things, it may be that you've forgotten why you're doing what you're doing. Sometimes tapping back into your reasons for carrying on will give you the strength to do so.
— *Richard Leider and David Shapiro*

December 18

Success

No matter how humble your work may seem, do it in the spirit of an artist, of a master. In this way, you lift it out of commonness and rob it of what would otherwise be drudgery.

— *Orison Marden*

Do the best you can in every task, no matter how unimportant it may seem at the time. No one learns more about a problem than the person at the bottom.
— *Sandra Day O'Connor*

It is not your business to succeed, but to do right; when you have done so, the rest lies with God.
— *C.S. Lewis*

Far better is to dare mighty things, to win glorious triumphs, even though checkered with failure, than to take rank with those poor spirits who neither enjoy much nor suffer much because they live in the gray twilight that knows not victory nor defeat.
— *Theodore Roosevelt*

December 19

Overcome Temptation

Ignoring a temptation is far more effective than fighting it. Once your mind is on something else, the temptation loses its power. So when temptation calls you on the phone, don't argue with it, just hang up.
— *Rick Warren*

If you have been tempted into evil, fly from it. It is not falling into the water, but lying in it, that drowns.
— *Anonymous*

In the greatest temptations, a single look to Christ, and the bare pronouncing of His name, suffices to overcome the wicked one, so it be done with confidence and calmness of spirit.

— *John Wesley*

The most effective defense against temptation is this: Shut your eyes.

— *Ibn Gabirol*

December 20

The Power of Commitment
Life rewards those who, having failed, and having failed over and over, still manage to move on. It is the decision to try again that will ultimately lead to a reward.

— *Fay Vincent, Jr.*

A man can transform faults into virtues if he but perseveres.

— *The Maggid of Dubno*

Most people achieved their greatest success one step beyond what looked like their greatest failure.

— *Brian Tracy*

Form a mental picture of a time or situation in which you never gave up, a time when you faced your fears and defeated them, or think of someone whose strength inspires you. Store that image in your mind and use it as an inner source of strength when you need to fortify your commitment and determination to achieve your goals and live your dreams.

— *Isiah Thomas*

December 21

Overcome Adversity
When obstacles arise, you change your direction to reach your goal, you do not change your decision to get there.
— *Zig Ziglar*

Obstacles cannot crush me. Every obstacle yields to stern resolve. He who is fixed to a star does not change his mind.
— *Leonardo da Vinci*

Obstacles are those frightful things you see when you take your eyes off the goal.
— *Hannah Moore*

People who are faced with obstacles should focus on the good things they can do and the positive way they can get around the obstacles. Don't focus on what the negatives might be and what you think the negatives could do to you, because you can always find a positive in any situation. If someone closes a door, work hard at finding another door.
— *Derek Jeter*

December 22

Faith

Faith is not believing that God can, but that God will.
— *Abraham Lincoln*

At the beginning of every act of faith, there is often a seed of fear.
— *Max Lucado*

Faith on a full stomach may be simply contentment – but if you have it when you're hungry, it's genuine.
— *Frank Clark*

When we look back at the faithfulness of God, we praise Him. When we look forward to God's faithfulness, we trust Him.
— *Ken Watters*

December 23

Mistakes

Mistakes are always forgivable, if one has the courage to admit them.
— *Bruce Lee*

The greatest mistake you can make in life is to be continually fearing you will make one.
— *Elbert Hubbard*

A man who refuses to admit his mistakes can never be successful. But if he confesses and forsakes them, he gets another chance.
— *Proverbs 28:13 (TLB)*

To err is human, to admit it, superhuman.
— *Doug Larson*

December 24

Today Is the Day

The ideal day never comes. Today is ideal for him who makes it so.

— *Horatio Dresser*

I will forget the happenings of the day that is gone, where they were good or bad, and greet the new sun with confidence that this will be the best day of my life.

— *Og Mandino*

One of the most tragic things I know about human nature is that all of us tend to put off living. We are all dreaming of some magical rose garden over the horizon – instead of enjoying the roses that are blooming outside our windows today.

— *Dale Carnegie*

Normal day, let me be aware of the treasure you are. Let me learn from you, love you, bless you before you depart. Let me not pass you by in quest of some rare and perfect tomorrow. Let me hold you while I may, for it may not always be so.

— *Mary Irion*

December 25

Become Wise
By associating with wise people you will become wise yourself.
— *Menander*

He who walks with the wise grows wise, but a companion of fools suffers harm.
— *Proverbs 13:20*

The art of being wise is the art of knowing what to overlook.
— *William James*

I will give you words and wisdom that none of your adversaries will be able to resist or contradict.
— *Luke 21:15*

December 26

Priorities

My cancer diagnosis prompted me to get my priorities straight, and fast. I realized that my health and family came first, my career second.

— *Joe Torre*

People often ask me now, "Zinger, is golf still as important to you as it was before you had cancer?" Golf is no longer at the top of my priority list. In fact, it runs a slow fourth. My priorities now are God, my family, my friends and golf.

— *Paul Azinger*

I learned more than I ever wanted to know last year. My baby's cancer strengthened me and my belief in what's important in life – my family, the kids.

— *Susie Redman*

Heather's illness made me think: Not that golf was unimportant to me, but that my petulance was ridiculous. Here I was getting angry about missing a green with a five-iron from 210 yards, and my wife had a life-threatening illness.

— *Darren Clarke*

December 27

Adversity

Great crises produce great men, and great deeds of courage.
— *John F. Kennedy*

Adversity is another way to measure the greatness of individuals. I never had a crisis that didn't make me stronger.
— *Lou Holtz*

It is by those who have suffered that the world has been advanced.
— *Leo Tolstoy*

When I hear my friends say they hope their children don't have to experience the hardships they went through – I don't agree. Those hardships made us what we are. You can be disadvantaged in many ways, and one way may be not having had to struggle.
— *William Batten*

December 28

The Treasure in Books
A book is a garden, an orchard, a storehouse, a party, a company by the way, a counselor, a multitude of counselors.
— *Henry Ward Beecher*

Books are the compasses and telescopes and sextants and charts which other men have prepared to help us navigate the dangerous seas of human life.
— *Jesse Bennett*

Books are the food of youth, the delight of old age, the ornament of prosperity, and the refuge and comfort of adversity.
— *Cicero*

Books are the quietest and most constant of friends, they are the most accessible and wisest of counselors and the most patient of teachers.
— *Charles Eliot*

December 29

Excuses

One of the chief differences between winners and losers is that winners see themselves as winning and losers generally give themselves a reason or an excuse to lose.

— *Roger von Oech*

The moment you blame anyone for anything, your relationship and your personal power deteriorate.

— *Brian Koslow*

People fail in direct proportion to their willingness to accept socially acceptable excuses for failure.

— *W. Steven Brown*

Don't succumb to excuses. Go back to the job of making the corrections and forming the habits that will make your goal possible.

— *Vince Lombardi*

December 30

Spiritual Life

I've never met anyone who became instantly mature. It's a painstaking process that God takes us through, and it includes such things as waiting, failing, losing and being misunderstood – each calling for extra doses of perseverance.

— *Charles Swindoll*

It is those who have a deep and real inner life who are best able to deal with the irritating details of outer life.

— *Evelyn Underhill*

There was often not enough time in the day to prepare thoroughly for an opponent. However, I learned over time that the more pressure I was under, the less I could afford to ignore my spiritual life.

— *Tom Osborne*

When we wait before the Lord and spend time with Him, the debris we have gathered during the hurried, busy hours of our day gets filtered out. With the debris out of the way, we are able to see things more clearly and feel God's nudgings more sensitively.

— *Charles Swindoll*

December 31

Human Beings

We are human beings, not human doings.
— *Rick Warren*

He is rich or poor according to what he is, not according to what he has.
— *Henry Ward Beecher*

Success is about having, and excellence is about being. Success is about having money and fame. But excellence is being the best you can be.
— *Mike Ditka*

Our worth comes from who we are, and not from what we do.
— *Dave Dravecky, pitcher who lost his pitching arm to cancer*

About the Author

David Young is a policy advisor to the governor of Texas. He received his Bachelor of Science in Business Administration degree, Summa Cum Laude, from the University of Arkansas and his Master of Business Administration degree from The University of Texas at Austin.

David grew up in Fort Smith, Arkansas. Both of his grandfathers were born before the Civil War. He and his wife, Christina, live in Round Rock, Texas. David has traveled extensively throughout the United States, Canada and Europe, and has visited South America, Asia and the Middle East.

Also by David Young

Breakthrough Power

Breakthrough Power for Mothers

Breakthrough Power for Fathers

Breakthrough Power for Christians

Breakthrough Power for Leaders

Breakthrough Power for Athletes

Breakthrough Power for Golfers

Great Funny Quotes

www.ingramcontent.com/pod-product-compliance
Lightning Source LLC
Chambersburg PA
CBHW032058090426
42743CB00007B/161